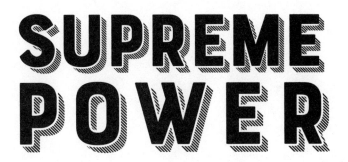

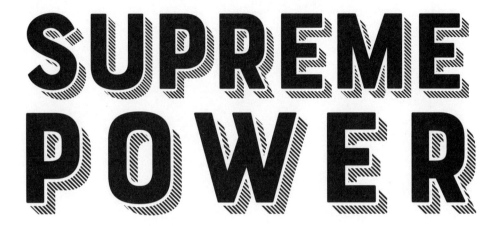

SUPREME POWER

7 | Pivotal Supreme Court Decisions That Had a Major Impact on America

TED STEWART

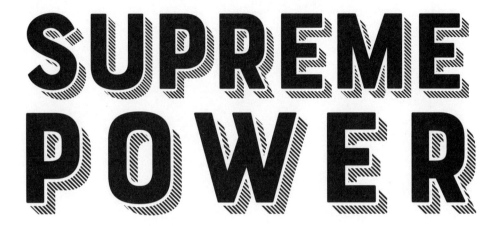

SHADOW
MOUNTAIN

Visit us at ShadowMountain.com

Library of Congress Cataloging-in-Publication Data

Names: Stewart, Ted, author.

Title: Supreme power : 7 pivotal Supreme Court decisions that had a major impact on America / Ted Stewart.

Description: Salt Lake City, Utah : Shadow Mountain, [2017] | Includes bibliographical references and index.

Identifiers: LCCN 2017017316 | ISBN 9781629723402 (hardbound : alk. paper)

Subjects: LCSH: United States. Supreme Court—History. | Political questions and judicial power— United States.

Classification: LCC KF8748 .S85 2017 | DDC 347.73/2609—dc23 LC record available at https:// lccn.loc.gov/2017017316

Printed in the United States of America

Publishers Printing, Salt Lake City, UT

10   9   8   7   6   5   4   3   2   1

To Tom, Ryan, Lena, Sandy, Patti, and all of my law clerks,
unheralded public servants all.

CONTENTS

CONTENTS

FOREWORD

U.S. CONGRESSMAN
CHRIS STEWART

Not long ago I found myself in Egypt for a few days. It was a busy trip and somewhat discouraging as I looked at the challenges facing this great nation, which has been a key U.S. ally for many years. The struggles that the Egyptian people were facing were enormous. Yet they seemed committed to finding a way to bring stability and prosperity to a country that is as rich in history as any in the world. I hoped they would be successful. It seemed that they deserved it.

As we drove through Cairo on the way to the airport, I stared out on what looked to be a dying city. From the elevated freeway, I could see the rooftops of the cement and wood apartments where garbage had been piled up because there was no more refuse collection going on. Passing by Tarik Square, I saw the burned-out remains of a government high-rise that had been damaged by gunfire, then set on fire by the fighting that had brought millions of protestors into the streets. The highway was packed with clanking taxies, motorcycles with three and four people holding on, rusty trucks, bikes, and occasional donkeys. I thought back on my interactions with the people. The Egyptians I had associated with were always friendly and optimistic, but they exuded a sense of realism as well. They had a challenge in rebuilding their country, and they knew that difficult days lie ahead.

An hour later, I found myself in the airport lounge waiting for the flight that would take me back home. Looking up, I saw a familiar face: a retired federal judge I had come to know in Washington, D.C. He sat down, and we started talking. "Why are you here?" I asked.

He had an interesting answer. And one that resonated with the same message that can be found in this book. More on that later.

★   ★   ★

As a U.S. Congressman, I have witnessed the executive branch suck up enormous power from the Congress. This is extremely concerning, for it upsets the delicate balance that our Founding Fathers intended between the three branches of government, leaving our President, a single individual, with far too much power and the people with less ability to govern themselves. But, as Ted Stewart points out in this book, we have also witnessed another great transfer of power away from the people. This transfer has moved power away from the Congress, away from the executive, even, and placed it within the chambers of the Supreme Court.

As the book relates, in 1922, a Supreme Court Justice was nominated by President Warren G. Harding and unanimously approved by the Senate on the same day. I actually laughed when I read this. It would be unimaginable today. And the reason is very simple: the Supreme Court has become so powerful, so omniscient, so authoritative and ever-present in our lives, that those nine Justices have become, in many ways, the most powerful individuals in the country. That being the case, is it any wonder that the opportunity to change the Court—which by extension would shift that balance of power within our nation—would come with enormous struggle and controversy?

Congressmen and Senators will come and go. They are constantly checked by the people in elections. Presidents must move on after no more than eight years. After they leave office, they often look back to see many of their priorities reversed or redirected by the next administration. But Supreme Court Justices enjoy a lifetime appointment, leaving them completely insulated from the will of the people. Their rulings cannot be challenged. They are very rarely reversed, and then only by a subsequent

Supreme Court ruling. There is no way to circumvent them or appeal their decisions to a higher authority.

They have come to rule over us and every aspect of our lives. As the late great Judge Antonin Scalia wrote, and as is quoted in this book, "It is not of special importance to me what the law says about marriage. It is of overwhelming importance, however, who it is that rules me. Today's decree says that my Ruler, and the Ruler of 320 million Americans coast-to-coast, is a majority of the nine lawyers on the Supreme Court. . . . This practice of constitutional revision by an unelected committee of nine, always accompanied (as it is today) by extravagant praise of liberty, robs the People of the most important liberty they asserted in the Declaration of Independence and won in the Revolution of 1776: the freedom to govern themselves" (*Obergefell v. Hodges,* 135 S.Ct. 2584, 2598 [2015]).

I believe that such a power is one that must be checked.

★　★　★

Back in Cairo, I listened as the retired judge explained how he had been in Egypt to train Egyptian judiciary officials on how to set up and maintain a proper judiciary system.

"It's important work," I offered.

"You have no idea," he replied. "If they don't have a proper judicial system, they have no hope of establishing a functioning government. They have no hope of freedom. No hope of stability. No hope of any future."

As he talked, I couldn't help but think that the same thing was true of my own government. It also explains why this book is so important.

The choice we have is very simple: divested power resting with the people, or, as the title of the book says, *Supreme Power* within the Court.

INTRODUCTION

"We are under a Constitution, but the
Constitution is what the judges say it is."

—*Charles Evans Hughes, then governor of New York and later
Chief Justice of the United States Supreme Court*

I n 1831, a young Frenchman named Alexis de Tocqueville came to the United States to study the American experiment in democracy, then in its infancy. Although his visit lasted only nine months, his powers of observation were so formidable that he was able to write what many consider the best book ever written about our system of government, *Democracy in America,* the first volume of which appeared in 1835. In that book he stated, "There is almost no political question in the United States that is not resolved sooner or later into a judicial question."[1] What was observably true to a visitor in the first half of the nineteenth century is unquestionably true to most Americans in the first half of the twenty-first century.

Presuming most, if not all, political questions become judicial questions, it makes sense to ask, "Who gets to decide the issues?" Or, more precisely, "Who gets the final word?" The honest answer is, "The Supreme Court of the United States."

Why is that so? Why are nine unelected men and women in fact the final deciders?

A Supreme Court Justice once answered that question, "We are not final because we are infallible, but we are infallible only because we are final."[2] This comment smacks of cynicism, but it is the candid truth and cannot be ignored. The Supreme Court is not unfailing because they are always right. In fact, the quoted Justice also acknowledged that if Supreme Court decisions were subject to further review by another group of judges, they would likely be reversed on occasion. But the fact is—there is no other court!

A decision by the Supreme Court interpreting the Constitution of the United States *cannot* be reversed except by an amendment to the Constitution or by a subsequent Supreme Court decision. Any Supreme Court interpretation of legislation passed by Congress cannot be undone except by changing the law or having the Supreme Court later change its mind. This is because in all such matters, the word of the United States Supreme Court is final. Was this truly what the Founders of our country envisioned?

THE FOUNDERS' VIEW

Above all else, those who founded this nation despised and feared tyranny. The tyranny that they dreaded can be explained by a simple, yet profound, formula:

- All people are born equal—that is, no one is born with the right to rule others, and no one is born to be ruled.
- Further, all people are born with rights bestowed by God, including specifically the right to life, liberty, and the "pursuit of happiness," which was understood to mean that men and women had the right to keep property they had honestly earned. These are sometimes referred to as natural rights.
- Because these rights come from God, they are inalienable and cannot be taken from people.
- The sole purpose of government is to secure and protect those fundamental, inalienable rights. To accomplish that end, men and women voluntarily create government, and they consent to be governed by that government.
- It is necessary for some rights or liberty to be voluntarily surrendered to government in order for that government to successfully protect the remainder or balance of those inalienable rights. For example, people must surrender a portion of their honestly earned income by paying taxes to fund a police department to protect life, liberty, and property from those who would take them by force.
- But, those natural rights and that liberty that remain after the creation of a government are to be jealously protected.
- If that government attempts to take more of the people's rights or liberty than have been voluntarily surrendered, that is tyranny.

In sum, tyranny is the involuntary loss of God-given rights or liberty.

The Founders of this great country had a vision for how tyranny was to be prevented in the nation to which they were giving birth. Most of their deliberations leading to the Constitution of the United States focused on that vision. They strove mightily to assure for their posterity that no one person or group of people, be they a President, a Congress, or a Court, could become so powerful that the people would lose their liberty.

Many of the giants of the Constitutional Convention of 1787—those most responsible for the Constitution of the United States—had studied and pondered upon the failed experiments in self-government dating back millennia. They were determined to avoid the mistakes of the past. The fruit of their effort was a masterfully crafted form of government with three separate but equal branches of government: an executive branch headed by the President, a legislative branch consisting of the House of Representatives and the Senate, and a judicial branch with the Supreme Court at the head.

Each of these branches of government would serve as a check on the other, and all three would serve as a counterbalance to curb the tendency for one or more to become too powerful. As James Madison wrote:

> An elective despotism was not the government we fought for; but one which should not only be founded on free principles, but in which the powers of government should be so divided and balanced among the several bodies of magistracy as that no one could transcend their legal limits without being effectually checked and restrained by the others.[3]

The Founders' plan also called for the national government to be checked by the states. They deliberately limited the power of the national government to those powers specifically enumerated or itemized in the Constitution. Their view was best expressed by Alexander Hamilton:

The State governments possess inherent advantages, which will ever give them an influence and ascendancy over the National Government, and will for ever preclude the possibility of federal encroachments. That their liberties, indeed, can be subverted by the federal head, is repugnant to every rule of political calculation.[4]

It was expected that this three-legged and multilayered sharing of power would thwart all forms of tyranny, despotism, or dictatorship.

The Founders foresaw their precious creation moving into the future guided by and shaped by "we, the people" through our elected officials. "Here, sir, the people govern!"[5]

It was a republic, after all!

It was an ingenious plan—the best the world has ever seen. The Founders themselves believed that it was the result of divine inspiration. It has survived for more than two and a quarter centuries.

But the Founders' thoughtfully crafted system seems not to have evolved as they had hoped. The balance has been severely upset. The checks have not quite worked. The America of today has not been shaped exclusively by the decisions of deliberative bodies of elected men and women. Rather, it is largely the creation of the Supreme Court of the United States. More precisely, it is the creation of the five members of the Supreme Court who have made up the majority of the Court in a handful of momentous Supreme Court decisions.

The possibility of this was not a surprise to all. In a series of letters published in a New York newspaper between October 1787 and April 1788, "Brutus" (a pseudonym commonly attributed to Judge Robert Yates, who had been a delegate to the 1787 Constitutional Convention) presented arguments to persuade the state of New York to reject ratification of the Constitution. These letters were among the most detailed of all those produced by the anti-Federalists and were a counterpoint to the letters being published in New York by James Madison, Alexander Hamilton, and John Jay that made up *The Federalist*—a collection of eloquent arguments in favor of the new Constitution.

In his Essay XI, Brutus focused on what he foresaw the danger to be:

> The real effect of this system of government, will therefore be brought home to the feelings of the people, through the medium of the judicial power. It is, moreover, of great importance, to examine with care the nature and extent of the judicial power, because those who are to be vested with it, are to be placed in a situation altogether unprecedented in a free country. They are to be rendered totally independent, both of the people and the legislature, both with respect to their offices and salaries. No errors they may commit can be corrected by any power above them, if any such power there be, nor can they be removed from office for making ever so many erroneous adjudications.[6]

Two months later, Brutus revisited the judiciary and expressed his fears even more forcefully:

> There is no power above them, to control any of their decisions. There is no authority that can remove them, and they cannot be controlled by the laws of the legislature. In short, they are independent of the people, of the legislature, and of every power under heaven. Men placed in this situation will generally soon feel themselves independent of heaven itself.[7]

Such bold language could not go unanswered. Alexander Hamilton accepted the task of replying to Brutus. Hamilton's arguments in support of Article III of the proposed Constitution, that article dealing with the judicial branch, are found in *The Federalist* in sections 78 to 83. In those essays, Hamilton contended that the judiciary was not the threat Brutus feared because judges had no control over either the purse (money) or the sword (the military). Hamilton also claimed that the judges had no ability to enforce their judgments by themselves, and that it would take either the legislative or the executive branches to enforce the judgments for the judges. Finally, he argued that the judges would only exercise "judgment" and could not impose their will.

The Madisons and the Hamiltons were sublimely confident that their judicial branch creation would truly exercise pure judgment and not impose its will. They believed that judges would be faithful to the intent of the Founders, and not practitioners of an "evolving" Constitution.

In even more basic terms, the Founders envisioned that federal judges would be like umpires calling balls and strikes, or like referees who were to keep the Team Congress and the Team Executive playing fair and square. It is arguable, however, that what has evolved is a system in which the courts have become more like dominant pitchers who can strike out every batter who steps into the batter's box, or like a 350-pound running back who scores a touchdown every time he is handed the ball.

In the end, Brutus lost the debate. But he proved to be the better prophet.

WHO GETS TO DECIDE WHO THE GREAT DECIDERS ARE?

If the Supreme Court has the final say on so many issues, it only makes sense that Americans ought to know as much about the Court as they can.

We should begin with the beginning. Article III of the Constitution of the United States is the source of the judicial power of the United States. It calls for the establishment of a Supreme Court and such other courts as the Congress may decide to create. It gives federal judges a lifetime term, subject only to impeachment by Congress for bad behavior. Article III insulates federal judges from reductions in their salary and also provides for the jurisdiction of the courts—that is, it describes what cases can be heard by the federal courts.

Although the Supreme Court is specifically called for in Article III of the Constitution, it was left to Congress to decide matters such as how many members of the Court there would be. Today there are nine members of the Supreme Court—a Chief Justice and eight Associate

Justices—but that has not always been true. On the original Supreme Court, which was the product of the legislation passed by Congress to implement Article III of the Constitution, the Judiciary Act of 1789, there were six Justices. In 1807, the number was increased to seven. The membership was again increased, to nine, in 1837, and to ten in 1863, but reduced to seven in 1866. Three years later it was increased to nine, where it has remained ever since. In 1937, President Franklin D. Roosevelt attempted to increase the membership to as many as fifteen in order to change the philosophical makeup of the Court. He was flailing about for anything that would remove the Court as a roadblock to his New Deal, but he failed.

Every instance of an increase or a decrease in the number of Justices occurred for a political reason: either to reward the President or political party in power with the ability to appoint new members, or to punish or prevent a President from naming members who might tip the balance.

When a vacancy on the Supreme Court occurs, usually through retirement but sometimes through the death of a Justice, the President is responsible for nominating a new member of the Court. That nominee must receive the approval of the United States Senate. Historically, the process of nomination and confirmation was relatively benign. A graphic example is the nomination in 1922 of George Sutherland, a former Senator from the state of Utah. Sutherland's friend and one-time Senate colleague, President Warren G. Harding, appointed Sutherland to the Supreme Court on September 5, 1922. He was confirmed the same day with no committee hearings—his name was sent directly to the floor of the Senate, where he received a unanimous vote. Sutherland was in England attending to government business and learned of his new position by way of a note he received from the President. In that note, President Harding referenced Sutherland's European travels, thanked the Sutherlands for inquiring after the health of Mrs. Harding, and then, almost as an afterthought, added:

> Since your departure for Europe you have been nominated
> and confirmed as a Justice of the United States Supreme Court.

I suppose you know all about this without me having taken the time to communicate with you. What pleases me more than anything else is that your nomination was received with unanimous satisfaction throughout the country.

Very sincerely yours,
Warren G. Harding[8]

It is inconceivable in this day that a Supreme Court nominee could be confirmed with such ease. That is true no matter how well qualified the nominee might be. This is simply because the Supreme Court has become so consequential in the governance of our nation that every nominee is subjected to incredible scrutiny and political maneuvering.

The power to nominate to the Supreme Court is found in Article II of the Constitution, that article dealing with the executive office—the President. How does a President decide whom to nominate?

There is no single set of criteria that Presidents rely on, and different considerations have been used by different Presidents throughout the history of our nation. There are no qualifications set forth by the Constitution or by law. One does not even have to be a lawyer to be named, although all Justices thus far have been trained in the law. Judicial philosophy, geographical balance, religion, political affiliation, and prior public service have all been factored into the decision. One expert suggests that modern-day Presidents rely on the opinions of public and political leaders, rankings by the American Bar Association, and input from sitting and former members of the Supreme Court.[9]

As the influence of the Supreme Court has exploded, more and more the judicial philosophy of the nominee becomes paramount. A President's ability to discern how a nominee is going to decide cases once he or she ascends to the Court, with a guarantee of thereafter being untouchable, is one of today's greatest tests of a President. Some have succeeded in properly assessing such. Many have not.

HOW THE COURT DECIDES

The Process. William Brennan served on the Supreme Court for twenty-four years, from 1956 to 1990. He was known to have asked his law clerks what the most important law at the Supreme Court was. He then answered his own question: "Five! The law of five! With five votes, you can do anything around here!"[10] Justice Brennan did not exaggerate: with five votes, any opinion or decision of the Supreme Court carries binding effect—and no less effect than if the vote had been 9–0.

All decisions of the Court are binding upon the parties to the immediate case decided and any others similarly situated. For example, if the Court decides a state statute is in violation of the United States Constitution, its decision invalidates not only that statute but all identical statutes that might be part of the statutory code of every other state.

Every binding decision is written and published to the world. These decisions are usually referred to as "opinions." The name should not be taken as signifying that they are simply suggestions or an expression of a sentiment by the Supreme Court. They are the law!

The Federal Court System. A detour might be necessary here to explain briefly the basic framework of the federal judiciary.

In the federal court system there are three levels of courts. The lowermost of the three are the district courts, where almost all cases originate, trials are held, and the factual record is generated. There are 94 district courts in the United States, with at least one in each state, and 673 district court judges.

The next level of courts is the Circuit Courts of Appeal. The country is divided into twelve geographic circuits, and every state belongs to one of the twelve circuits. In addition, there is a thirteenth court of appeals, the Court of Appeals for the Federal Circuit, which hears appeals involving patent law, the court of international trade, and the court of federal claims. There are 179 circuit court judges sitting on these circuit courts, with a low number of 6 in the First Circuit and 29 in the largest, the Ninth Circuit. The circuit courts normally hear appeals with panels consisting of three circuit judges.

Any decision made by a district court can be appealed to a circuit court—thus, any litigant in the federal court system is guaranteed at least two chances to win: they have the opportunity to convince either a district court judge or jury, or a three-judge circuit court panel, of the rightness of their position. In a typical year, the circuit courts collectively hear and decide as many as 27,000 cases.

Finally, at the highest level is the Supreme Court. Besides hearing appeals from the federal circuit courts, the Supreme Court also entertains appeals from the highest courts in the fifty states. Obviously, the nine members of the Supreme Court cannot hear every appeal from the circuit courts and state supreme courts. In an average year, approximately 7,000 to 8,000 petitions or requests are submitted to the Supreme Court asking it to hear appeals.

HOW CASES GET TO THE SUPREME COURT

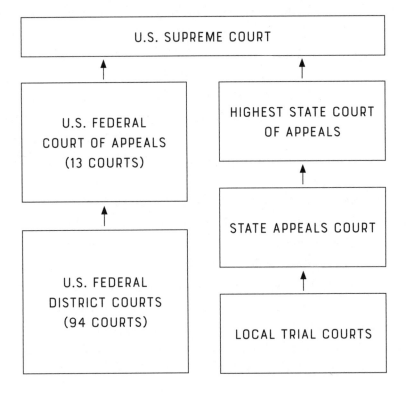

Accepting an Appeal. The Supreme Court gets to pick and choose which cases it will hear and decide. The "Rule of Four" applies: four of the nine Justices have to agree to accept the appeal. Normally, only 80 to 100 of the 7,000 to 8,000 petitions are heard and decided by the Court during a term of the Court, which runs from the first Monday in October until the end of June.

How the Justices choose which appeals they hear is, as former Chief Justice William Rehnquist once observed, "a rather subjective decision, made up in part of intuition and in part of legal judgment."[11] However, there are certain considerations that most Court observers believe the Justices use in deciding which cases to take.

The Justices strive to promote uniformity and consistency in the law. Therefore, if different circuit courts have decided major issues differently, the Supreme Court may take a case to eliminate that split of opinion. Many people do not realize that if one circuit court has decided a matter one way, and another circuit decides it another way, those who reside within the states that make up the first circuit are subject to a different law than those in the states covered by the other circuit.

A recent example will demonstrate this: Two men lived on opposite sides of the Missouri River but both within the Kansas City metropolitan area. Both men had been convicted of sex offenses that required them to register as sex offenders under federal law. Both men flew out of the Kansas City International Airport to the same international destination. Neither of them had updated their sex offender registration information. Both were prosecuted for failing to do so. The man who resided in Missouri, which is in the Eighth Circuit, was found not to have violated the federal law. The man who resided in Kansas, in the Tenth Circuit, was found guilty for the exact same conduct.

Such "circuit splits" usually motivate the Supreme Court to take and decide a case to eliminate the division.

The Court will also look favorably to taking a case that involves an interpretation of federal law that has not yet been decided by the Supreme Court.

It is also recognized that when a truly major controversy erupts that can only be decided by the highest court in the land, the Supreme Court will take that case. An example would be the contested presidential election of 2000.

Another consideration would be whether four Justices believe that a lower court decision has failed to apply a prior Supreme Court decision, or if a lower court has departed from the accepted and usual course of judicial proceedings.

These criteria for deciding to accept appeals are not exhaustive, nor are they binding on the Court. Often, Court observers are truly surprised when a case is accepted for review, but they are even more often surprised when the Court refuses a high-profile appeal. The Court does not have to explain why it refuses to accept an appeal. Those who are refused are usually left to wonder.

Making a Decision. It would be wrong for anyone to assume that the ultimate role of the Supreme Court is to assure that justice is done in every case. As comforting as it would be to believe that in the end all injustice will be rooted out by the Supreme Court, that is impossible—the numbers simply do not permit that to be the Court's ultimate goal or responsibility.

Once a case has been accepted, it is put on the Court's calendar for oral argument. Some time before that argument, the parties file written briefs with the Court in which they summarize their arguments, refer to or cite those cases that they believe are precedent, provide overall guidance to the Court, and generally try to persuade the Court to side with them. These written briefs are of great importance because the time allotted for oral argument is very short.

Each Justice prepares for oral argument in his or her own way. Some have their law clerks prepare memoranda containing digests of the briefs, the law clerks' analysis of the law and arguments, and a recommendation for the Justice as to how they believe the case should be decided. Other Justices read the briefs themselves and require their law clerks to do the same. They then focus their minds through discussions, formal and informal, with their clerks.

Oral arguments occur in the Supreme Court courtroom. The time allotted to each side is usually only thirty minutes. Rarely does an attorney representing a side have the luxury of making prepared remarks for that full half an hour—normally the bulk of the time is spent responding to questions from the Justices. In very rare cases, arguments are permitted for longer times, occasionally several hours, or even days if the Court considers the case important enough.

Within days of the oral argument, the Justices meet in what they call a conference. It has been the practice to begin the conference with every Justice shaking hands with every other Justice, a blunt reminder that differences that might be bared during the upcoming meeting are legal and judicial, not personal. Only the nine Justices attend the conference. There are no law clerks or secretaries—only the Justices.

Consideration of the case begins with the Chief Justice summarizing the case and then informing his colleagues how he is going to vote. The remaining Justices, in order of seniority, then do the same. They do so without being interrupted; there are neither questions asked nor reactions expressed in reply to each Justice's statement. After the last Justice has spoken, it is evident what the outcome of the case will be.

Remarkably, there is little interplay or discussion among the Justices in the conference. Each Justice has read the same briefs, heard the same oral argument, and presumably is equally competent to decide the case for herself or himself. For the most part, each Justice simply states his or her position. Decision making is individual, not collective.

Dissent is not discouraged. Consensus is not demanded. As long as there are at least five of the Justices who agree with an outcome, a decision has been reached.

The next step is the assigning of one Justice to write the opinion for the majority. If the Chief Justice is with the majority, he makes the assignment. If the Chief Justice is with the minority, the most senior Associate Justice in the majority makes the assignment.

Once a draft opinion has been prepared by the assigned Justice, it is then circulated to all the other Justices. If a Justice agrees in total with the opinion, he or she informs the author of his or her desire to join in the opinion. If a Justice has a suggestion as to how to make the opinion better, he or she will suggest such in writing to the author. Normally, changes have to be made in the draft opinion to get the required five votes in support. In a landmark or controversial case, draft upon draft may be necessary to obtain a majority of five Justices to agree. The decisions reached earlier in the conference are not finalized or announced until this written opinion is issued.

On occasion, instead of agreeing with the language of a majority opinion, Justices may agree only with the outcome and will write concurring opinions to express their own justification for that outcome.

Those who are in dissent are also writing and circulating their dissenting opinions. Sometimes multiple dissenting opinions are published.

It is worth noting that after the initial conference, where the positions are stated by each Justice, the Court never again comes together to discuss the case or opinions. It is the practice that all interaction thereafter is through the circulation of written opinions and letters or memos joining or suggesting changes. Personal discussions with a fellow Justice about a case are extremely rare and may take place only once or twice each year.

Once the full opinion is finalized, including any concurring or dissenting opinions, it is verbally announced in the courtroom and published to the world.[12]

The Judicial Philosophy. There have been many efforts to brand the judicial philosophy of Justices of the Supreme Court. To simplify discussion in this book, and because the author accepts the uncomplicated view that there are actually only two distinct judicial philosophies relied upon by Supreme Court Justices when interpreting the Constitution of the United States, only two philosophies will be referenced.

The first philosophical type of Justice will be referred to as an "Originalist." An Originalist is a Justice who believes that the law serves the community best when it is as predictable and stable as possible—especially when it comes to interpreting the Constitution. Originalists believe that such predictability and stability are best achieved when one ties constitutional interpretation to a consistent point of reference. Thus, they always begin their interpretation of the Constitution based upon the language of the document itself. When the language of the document affords more than one interpretation, if those interpretations conflict, Originalists look to what the language meant to the people who wrote the document and to those who ratified the original Constitution or the amendments to it. Originalists believe that the voice of the people, as expressed through legislation passed by their elected representatives, should not be overturned by the courts unless there is evidence that such legislation violates the language or the intention of the Founders. They believe that the Constitution should be immune, as much as possible, to the shifting tides of public opinion. They believe that if public opinion solidifies around a change in the Constitution, the amendment process is available to make that change.

The second type of Justices will be referred to as "Living Constitutionalists." They too believe in predictability and stability, but they do not believe those are best achieved through reliance on the words of a document over two hundred years old, nor on the intent of those who crafted it. In sum, Living Constitutionalists believe that the Constitution must be interpreted to reflect present-day values and must adapt to present-day challenges and needs. To determine what those values, challenges, and needs are, adherents to this judicial philosophy rely on their own intellectual, moral, and personal perceptions and beliefs.

In applying either judicial philosophy, there is a certain level of subjective decision making involved. In the latter, however, the Justice allows himself or herself much more latitude to do what he or she thinks is the right outcome, what the Constitution ought to mean, with less restraint by what the Founders may have believed it to mean.[13]

WHY THIS BOOK?

This book was written to explain how and in what ways the country we live in today has been shaped, molded, and fashioned by the judicial branch. It tells the stories of seven cases that made their way to the highest court in the land and what the Court, often in a 5–4 split, decided.

We will begin with the case that made all the rest of the cases happen—*Marbury v. Madison* (1803)—in which the Supreme Court established itself as the final word on what is or is not constitutional.

We follow with the case of *Plessy v. Ferguson* (1896), the Supreme Court decision that ended the efforts in the last half of the nineteenth century to integrate African-Americans into mainstream society, sanctioned state-sponsored segregation, and explains to some extent why our nation remains racially divided so many decades later.

The case of *Lochner v. New York* (1905) is considered the birth of the judicial doctrine that allows unelected judges wide discretion to decide what the government can or cannot regulate. Although that case dealt with the question of what hours a baker could work, it is the genesis of the abortion and same-sex marriage decisions of decades later.

Next we will explore *Wickard v. Filburn* (1942), a case that opened the floodgates of federal regulation of commerce and business and has been used to justify the explosion of federal criminal laws and regulations.

A limited interweaving of religion and government existed with little criticism until the case of *Everson v. Board of Education* (1947). In that case, the Supreme Court decision discovered the previously unknown wall between religion and government that has subsequently been used to remove religion from the public sphere.

A battle cry of the American Revolution was "no taxation without representation!" Yet in *Missouri v. Jenkins* (1990), the Supreme Court authorized an unelected federal judge to raise taxes on the citizens of a school district in Missouri in order to carry out his dreams and visions for a desegregated public school district.

Finally, we explore the phenomenon of "social reformation without representation" by virtue of Supreme Court decisions such as *Obergefell v. Hodges* (2015) that have upended the societal, cultural, and moral norms of American society.

Among other reasons, this book has been written to help the reader understand why the entire nation finds itself breathlessly awaiting the major Supreme Court decisions often handed down at the end of its annual term in June of each year. It is also hoped that the reader may more fully understand why the battles over who is appointed to the Supreme Court have in some respects come to overshadow the contests for control of either the White House or the Congress.

NOTES

Epigraph: In Pritchett, "Divisions of Opinion."
1. De Tocqueville, *Democracy*, 257.
2. *Brown v. Allen*, 344 U.S. 443 (1953), 540 (Jackson, J. concurring).
3. James Madison, in Hamilton, Jay, and Madison, *Federalist*, 270.
4. Alexander Hamilton, speech delivered at the New York Ratifying Convention, June 20, 1788; in Spalding, *Almanac*, 154.
5. Ibid., 178.
6. In Ketcham, *Anti-Federalist Papers*, 293.
7. Ibid., 305.
8. This letter is among the Sutherland papers to be found in the Library of Congress.
9. Abraham, *Justices*, 18–19.
10. Toobin, *Nine*, 84–85.
11. Rehnquist, *Supreme Court*, 234.
12. This overview of how the Court reaches its decisions comes primarily from Rehnquist, *Supreme Court*. Other sources for insight into the operations of the Court come from Woodward and Armstrong, *Brethren*; Tushnet, *Court Divided*; Greenburg, *Supreme Conflict*; and Toobin, *Nine*.
13. For a more detailed discussion of judicial philosophy, see Bork, *Tempting*, and Scalia, *Matter of Interpretation*.

CHAPTER ONE

HOW THE SUPREME COURT BECAME SUPREME

MARBURY V. MADISON (1803)

"William Marbury has been saved from historical obscurity only by the fact that he was the plaintiff in the most famous case ever decided by the United States Supreme Court."

—*Chief Justice William Rehnquist*

I n the long history of the United States Supreme Court, of the thousands of people whose cases have been heard by that Court, only one person has a portrait hanging next to that of his legal antagonist on the walls of the Supreme Court Building. That person is William Marbury, whose portrait hangs next to that of James Madison in the "John Marshall Room" of the Supreme Court.[1]

Why this is so is what this chapter is about.

WASHINGTON, D.C., CIRCA 1800

Washington, D.C., was not much of a place in 1800.

Our nation's first capital was in the country's largest city, New York City. It was there that George Washington took the oath of office in 1789. By the time of his second inauguration, in 1793, the capital had moved to another major metropolis: Philadelphia, Pennsylvania. However, as of that date an entirely new and permanent location for the capital had been decided upon—a ten-mile-square piece of ground on the Potomac River straddling Virginia and Maryland. That location was fixed as a result of a grand compromise. In exchange for supporting Secretary of the Treasury Alexander Hamilton's financial scheme of having the federal government assume the debts incurred by the states during the American Revolution (an action supported by the banks and financiers from the northern states), the placement of the permanent capital in a southern location had been agreed to.

George Washington had personally chosen the site and hired a Frenchman who had served in the Continental Army, Pierre Charles L'Enfant, to lay out the new city. His plans included a stately Capitol Building on a hill overlooking the flatlands and swamps extending down to the Potomac River. It called for a long, open mall leading from that building to the river, and broad avenues radiating out from the Capitol. The residence for the President was located a mile and a half from the Capitol Building on Pennsylvania Avenue.

Grand in scheme and design, the scope of the project would not become visible to the general public for many decades.

In 1800, the population of Washington, D.C., was about three thousand. It was little more than a place where trees had been cleared, leaving an enormous space with lots of tree stumps, a few scattered buildings, and all of it surrounded by wilderness. The houses were few and far between. Many were simple cabins. There were a handful of taverns, seven or eight boardinghouses, one tailor, one printer, one washing woman, and one grocery shop.

The red clay soil made travel miserable when wet and dusty when dry. Swamps were breeding grounds for mosquitos.

The wing of the Capitol that was to house the Senate was completed, but the wing that was to become the home of the House of Representatives was not finished. The rotunda had yet to receive a roof.

The city was surrounded by dense forests, and even the primary roads leading to it were more like trails. Travel from the nearest large city, Baltimore, Maryland, was not easy. When Abigail Adams was traveling to join her husband, President John Adams, in the new capital, her entourage got lost and traveled nine miles in the wrong direction.

Nearby was the village of Georgetown. Abigail described it as a dirty hole, and she did not have much kind to say about its residents. The city of Alexandria adjoined the new capital city on the south.

Churches were nonexistent in the area in 1800. Whether for convenience or out of necessity, by 1802 church services were being conducted in the House of Representatives. President Thomas Jefferson was a regular attendee at those services, as was his successor, James Madison. The House of Representatives would be used for religious services until after the American Civil War.[2]

The official move from Philadelphia to Washington, D.C., had taken place in June of 1800. It was not really much of a move, for there were only 130 employees of the government of the United States at that time. It was a tiny community.

President John Adams had to stay in a boardinghouse until he moved into the still-unfinished White House in November of 1800.

But his stay was going to be a very short one.[3]

THE PRESIDENTIAL ELECTION OF 1800:
THE MOST BITTER ELECTION IN HISTORY?

There has never been an assemblage of men to equal the Founders. One cannot look at what they created without being amazed. But, like all men, they were very, very human. Jealousies, intrigues, and rivalries were not uncommon. As united as they were against a common enemy, Great Britain, that unity evaporated as the new nation emerged from its birth into its infancy. Personal relationships became quite complicated.

One of the most curious examples was the relationship between John Adams and Thomas Jefferson. Their friendship took root at the First Continental Congress. It was during that Congress that Adams became known as "the voice of the Revolution" and Jefferson "the pen." It was Adams who suggested that Jefferson write the Declaration of Independence, thereby gifting Jefferson with the opportunity to author one of the greatest documents in all political history.

They suffered abroad together as the primary diplomats for the new country, dutifully representing the United States in the years after the Revolution. They were both part of the George Washington administration: Adams as Vice President and Jefferson as Secretary of State. They corresponded incessantly.

Their friendship suffered as Adams remained a committed Federalist while Jefferson and James Madison quietly formed an alliance that would lead to the creation of a second political party, the Republican Party. This development was not foreseen by most of the Founders. The emergence of political parties was a surprise to these wise men. Perhaps they had simply underestimated the citizens of their new nation as well as themselves personally.

In 1796, Jefferson ended up running for President against Adams. The Federalists were not yet to be dislodged, Jefferson lost, and under the system then in place (until passage of the Twelfth Amendment in 1804), he became Adams's Vice President.

The four years of Adams's presidency were tumultuous ones. He and his Vice President were to disagree on just about everything. Adams and the Federalists worked to assure a strong national government, while Jefferson favored continued empowerment of the states and more democracy for the people. In foreign policy, Adams continued Washington's efforts to reestablish ties to the mother country, Great Britain. Jefferson leaned toward the French, even supporting the French Revolution long after it had degenerated into blood and anarchy.

This well-known sympathy for French revolutionary fervor led Adams and the Federalists who controlled Congress to believe foolish rumors, such as one suggesting that the Republicans wanted to overthrow the Federalist government by force. In fear, the Congress passed the infamous Alien and Sedition Acts. One of these acts made it a crime to publish anything against the government that could be considered false or malicious. Another gave the President authority to deport anyone deemed to be a danger to the American system. President Adams had not suggested the legislation, but he did sign it. A significant number of criminal prosecutions were initiated for violations of these Congressional acts.

It is very difficult for one looking backward to understand how the protections enshrined in the First Amendment to the Constitution, freedom of speech and of the press, could be disregarded just a few years later. It is worth remembering, however, that the young United States felt very threatened by European powers—Great Britain and France particularly. The acts also reflected the increasing shrillness of public debate, most of which was being conducted in the press. Still, these acts were abominable, then and now. They generated an incredible amount of animosity toward the Federalists and drove many Americans to support the emerging party of Jefferson.

The Republicans believed these acts were targeted at their party generally and at Thomas Jefferson specifically. The rancor and acrimony among the nation's political leaders only increased.

Jefferson used the last two years of his Vice Presidency encouraging, indirectly, his own candidacy. He urged others to write and publish criticism of Adams and the Federalists, he supported Republican newspapers, and he engaged in intrigues with James Madison and others disgruntled with the Federalists and the President.

As the election of 1800 approached, the Federalist Party under John Adams was on the decline, and the Republicans under Jefferson were on the ascent. Besides criticism from the outside, the Federalists were being torn apart internally, with Alexander Hamilton expressing great disappointment with President Adams in a well-publicized writing—calling him eccentric and responsible for nearly destroying the nation.

As for the nation as a whole, it was experiencing steady growth. It now consisted of sixteen states, and its population had doubled since 1776 to more than five million. The territory to the west was being settled. This created challenges for the political contenders. It would still be several decades before it would be deemed proper for candidates to campaign personally. Most electioneering was conducted through hyper-partisan newspapers, pamphlets, and occasional mass meetings. The candidates for both parties were selected by Congressional caucus: John Adams and Charles Pinckney for the Federalists and Thomas Jefferson and Aaron Burr for the Republicans.

There were issues that divided the parties, but they were likely of little import compared to the personal assaults flung about by both sides. There is evidence that principals in both parties consciously decided to put "principle aside" and to go for the jugular.

From the Federalists came the message that Jefferson was an atheist and that his election would show that the nation was in open defiance of God. He was portrayed as not only unfaithful to, but an enemy of,

Christianity. It was suggested that he was a libertine and had slave mistresses, that all morality would be destroyed by a Jefferson victory, and that the chastity of wives and daughters would be lost.

One newspaper posed a key question "to be asked by every American, laying his hand on his heart," as: "Shall I continue in allegiance to God—and a religious President; Or impiously declare for Jefferson—and No God!!!"[4]

Further, Federalists proclaimed, Jefferson was too much of a supporter of the French Revolutionists who were still wreaking death and havoc in France. The Federalists asserted that the Republicans were out to destroy both property and religion, as was happening in France, and that they wanted to make the United States a satellite of France. The Federalists claimed that a Republican victory would reduce the United States to a land of groans, and tears, and blood.

From the Republicans came claims that Adams was an autocrat and that the Federalists wanted to make the United States a plutocracy governed by the wealthy of the Northern states. The Alien and Sedition Acts were held up as clear evidence of the Federalists' tyrannical laws. It was claimed that war was inevitable if Adams were reelected. They also contended that the Federalists were declared fans of the British crown and were willing to make the United States an outpost of Great Britain again.

Personal attacks were common and unusually vicious even by modern standards. For example, John Adams was later informed that the reason he had lost the state of Pennsylvania was because it was rumored among the large German population there that he had imported two mistresses, one French and the other German, and that he had sent the German mistress away. Another rumor had it that he had sent his vice-presidential running mate to London to return with four mistresses for the two of them to share. Jefferson's supporters alleged that Adams was insane, a lunatic, and quite mad.

Despite the ugliness of the campaign, or perhaps because of it, public interest in the election was intense. Upwards of 70 percent of eligible voters showed up to vote in some areas. The election for President was very close and ultimately it was thrown into the House of Representatives for the members there to decide. It took 36 ballots and until February 17, 1801, for Jefferson to emerge victorious.

As aggressive as the assaults on both sides were, they were apparently sincere. When Jefferson emerged the victor, he genuinely believed that he had saved the country. In turn, the Federalists were convinced that the nation was lost.

Besides losing the Presidency, the Federalists were soundly defeated in the Congressional elections, and the Republicans took control of both houses of Congress. Once the President and new Congress took over in March, the Federalists were eliminated from power in both the legislative and executive branches.

The Federalists were finished as a political party—but not as a force in our nation.[5]

THE UNDELIVERED COMMISSION

John Adams was not happy to see his colleague of nearly a quarter of a century replace him, and he was not going to end his presidency gracefully. He refused to attend Jefferson's inauguration on March 4—in fact, he left Washington at four in the morning, eight hours before Thomas Jefferson was to become the third President. He did, however, have the courtesy to send a letter to Jefferson, informing him that the horses and carriages at the White House were the property of the United States and therefore there was no need for Jefferson to supply his own.

But missing the swearing in of his successor was the least of the insults aimed at Jefferson and his Republican Party. Just three weeks before Jefferson was sworn in, the Federalists, sitting as a lame-duck Congress, passed legislation known as the Judiciary Act of 1801. That legislation reduced the number of Supreme Court Justices from six to five—just to keep Jefferson from having an appointment to the Court. (This part of the act was reversed the next year.) It also created new district courts and expanded the number of circuit courts and justice of the peace positions. In total, it gave the outgoing President Adams fifty-eight judicial positions to fill with Federalist judges—this to complement the existing judiciary, which consisted entirely of Federalists.

John Adams named his judges the day before Jefferson was to be inaugurated. The nominations were approved by the lame-duck Federalist Congress the next morning, the day of the inauguration. This group became known, quite appropriately, as the "Midnight Judges."

To complete the process, written commissions had to be delivered to the new judges. This responsibility fell upon John Marshall, who was then serving the dual role of Supreme Court Chief Justice and Secretary of State. He was a busy man, and somehow four of the commissions were never delivered.

The naming of the Midnight Judges was an act that offended Thomas Jefferson mightily. He was later to say that of all the differences and quarrels he had with John Adams, this was the one that wounded him the most. Jefferson ordered that the undelivered commissions remain undelivered.

One of those Midnight Judges was William Marbury, a loyal Federalist. He was confirmed by the Senate on the day of Jefferson's swearing in, but he could not take the oath of office until his commission was delivered. Marbury was thus unable to function as a justice of the peace. He sued the new Secretary of State, James Madison, for delivery of the commission.

Marbury's case was not heard until February of 1803 because the new Republican Congress set about almost immediately to repeal the Judiciary Act of 1801and prohibited the Supreme Court from sitting until that date in order to assure that the Court did not declare the repeal of the Judiciary Act unconstitutional.

Thus, a Supreme Court made up of Federalist Justices was set to hear a case brought by a Federalist appointee, appointed by a Federalist President, and naming the new Secretary of State, James Madison, perhaps the most prominent Republican next only to Thomas Jefferson, as the defendant.

THE FEDERALIST COURTS

The seat of the federal government had moved from Philadelphia to Washington, D.C., in June of 1800. Planning for that move had been under way for a decade. However, it was not until January of the next year that it suddenly occurred to anyone that there was no place for the Supreme Court to meet when it began its term in February. Scrambling, officials snatched a small committee room, about 24 by 30 feet, from the Senate, and told the Supreme Court to conduct its business in that room. It did so for the next eight years.

This seeming affront was not unusual for the Supreme Court. It was consistent with the treatment of the federal judiciary generally since adoption of the Constitution eleven years earlier.

In that eleven-year period, the Supreme Court saw four Chief Justices come and go. The first, John Jay, served for six years, but while serving took time off to run twice for governor of New York. He also accepted an invitation from President Washington to travel to England to help negotiate a treaty with Great Britain. The next Chief Justice, John Rutledge, served for less than one year, and during that time only two cases were decided by the Court. The third Chief Justice, Oliver Ellsworth, served for almost five years. He too was sent off to Europe during his tenure to serve as the head of a delegation to France.

In total, prior to John Marshall's Court, the Supreme Court had decided only twelve cases. But this inactivity and apparent indolence was just what many of the Founders anticipated—and what most of them truthfully wanted.

The question of the need for a national judiciary was not open-and-shut to many of the Founders. Under the governing system prior to the Constitution of 1787, the Articles of Confederation, there were no federal courts except for a single court created to deal with admiralty or maritime issues. To the extent national law was enforced, it was enforced by state courts. It was discovered, however, that such local courts were sometimes loath to trigger the anger of their fellow state citizens when it came to enforcing unpopular federal laws. For example, the treaty that ended

31

the war with Great Britain allowed British creditors to collect debts owed by American businesses and individuals. To do so, those creditors usually had to go to court. The state courts did not take warmly to being called upon to enforce such a treaty right.

Among many early Americans, there was a great fear of a federal court system. This was true for many reasons, including concerns that federal courts would upend the power of state courts, might pose a threat to the jury system, and would weaken the power of states to resist federal mandates and power generally.

Still, at the Constitutional Convention of 1787, it was agreed that a federal court system was necessary. The Constitution provided for the creation of a Supreme Court. However, the question of how many lower courts there would be and what types of cases they could hear and decide was all left to the judgment of the Congress to assemble after the Constitution's ratification.

That Congress dipped its toe ever so lightly into the controversial subject of federal courts. The Judiciary Act of 1789 gave life to the Supreme Court. It also created a handful of the lowest of the courts, the district courts. As to the jurisdiction for those courts, it was limited almost exclusively to hearing cases between citizens of two different states. However, the amount of money in controversy between those litigants had to be at least $500, the equivalent of roughly $13,500 today. Thus, the likelihood of a civil dispute being heard in federal court was slim. There were practically no federal criminal statutes. The district courts were not even given jurisdiction to hear all the cases involving enforcement of federal laws.

More jurisdiction was given to the circuit courts that were to be made up of one district court judge and two Supreme Court Justices. In order for these circuit courts to operate, the Supreme Court Justices had to "ride circuit," that is, travel to each of the states to conduct trials. But the 1789 Act limited the number of times the federal circuit courts could meet. Along with the limitations on jurisdiction, this removed the threat that these federal courts would usurp the preeminence of the state courts.

The primary difference between the Federalists and the Republicans was over the intended power of the federal government. In the last desperate act to assure a more vibrant and potent national government, the lame-duck Federalist Congress had passed the Judiciary Act of 1801, which created sixteen new circuit court judges. The circuit-riding Supreme Court Justices were most grateful for that. The act also lowered the threshold for federal civil court jurisdiction to $100. Finally, the act vested in the federal courts the authority to hear and decide all questions of federal law. When the Republicans took control of Congress, they undid much of the 1801 Judiciary Act, including abolishing the new circuit court positions.

It was this environment of political warfare and active strife regarding the existence and authority of the federal courts into which Chief Justice John Marshall waded in 1803.[6]

THE CHIEF JUSTICE

Who was this John Marshall, the man who is uniformly acknowledged to have been the most important Chief Justice in the history of the United States?

Marshall was born in Virginia in 1755. He was a distant cousin of Thomas Jefferson through his mother. His father was involved in public life. At age twenty, Marshall joined his father's militia unit to fight the British and was later an officer under George Washington, his father's close friend.

He was with Washington at Valley Forge. It was his experiences as a soldier, seeing the weak national government fail in its efforts to outfit its army, that led Marshall to the Federalist political party. He believed that the national government had to be strong enough to meet certain basic needs of its citizens, including providing for the defense of the nation.

Marshall was close enough to Washington to be deemed his protégé. He was part of Washington's headquarters staff, and such proximity to the future President was to prove valuable to Marshall's career.

Upon his discharge, Marshall studied law. His prior education was one year at a boarding school and one year under a tutor. He was brilliant enough that after just one year at William and Mary, he was able to begin the practice of law and proved to be successful in that endeavor.

He began a political career at age twenty-seven, when he was elected to the Virginia General Assembly. As a well-known Federalist, he was in the minority in Virginia, but he was still able to play a significant role at the 1788 Virginia Ratifying Convention. His primary role was to defend the federal judiciary under the Constitution. Specifically, he argued that the federal judiciary would be a defender of the rights of the people through serving as a check on Congressional power. He specifically recognized and reasoned that the federal courts would have the power to declare void a law passed by Congress that was in violation of the Constitution. Thus, fifteen years before the fact, John Marshall publicly recognized the right of judicial review.

Marshall practiced law during the Washington years and resisted efforts to enlist him in public service. However, he succumbed to entreaties from President John Adams and served as an emissary for Adams to the French government. This was the beginning of his service at the national level.

In 1799, at the personal urging of George Washington, Marshall ran for and was elected to the House of Representatives. He immediately became a source of influence in the Congress because of his moderate views and native intelligence. He remained loyal to John Adams when many of the Federalists abandoned Adams at the urging of Alexander Hamilton. He was named Adams's Secretary of State in May of 1800.

The following year, after it was clear that John Adams would be turned out of the Presidency, Adams desperately wanted to appoint someone to fill the position of Chief Justice upon the resignation of Oliver Ellsworth. His first choice was his old friend John Jay, who had served before, as the nation's first Chief Justice. Jay declined. Marshall later related that he and Adams were discussing the matter when Adams turned to him and asked, "Whom shall I nominate now?" Marshall replied that he did not know, upon which Adams declared, "I believe

I must nominate you." One great historian has asserted that in its far-reaching importance to the United States, this appointment was second only to Adams's appointment of George Washington to command the Continental Army twenty-five years earlier.[7] John Adams gave those two decisions a different prioritization: "My gift of John Marshall to the people of the United States was the proudest act of my life."[8]

John Adams wanted someone as Chief Justice to serve for a long time. When appointed, Marshall was forty-five years old. He was to serve in the position for over thirty-four years.

One month after he was sworn in, as a renowned Federalist, he was asked by his cousin Thomas Jefferson to administer the presidential oath to him. Marshall welcomed the opportunity to show that the passage of power from the Federalist Party to the Republican Party could occur without rancor. He did not trust his cousin, but he had bowed to the verdict of the people.[9]

THE IMPEACHMENT

The Republican Party under Thomas Jefferson was not fond of the federal courts. This animosity was sparked by a number of factors but included the fact that almost all federal judges were Federalists. Another reason was the willingness of some of those judges to enforce laws that were truly abominable to the Republicans, specifically the Alien and Sedition Acts.

This enmity led to Republican efforts to diminish the influence of federal courts. Those efforts included the repeal of the 1801 Judiciary Act and the suspending of the entire 1802 term of the Supreme Court by the new Republican Congress. One final effort that must be mentioned was the impeachment of Judge John Pickering.

After its yearlong ban, the Supreme Court was scheduled to return to business in February of 1803. Just a few days before the Court was to begin its term, President Jefferson sent a written message to the House of Representatives suggesting that the House consider impeaching a federal district court judge, John Pickering of New Hampshire.

Pickering had been named to the district court by George Washington in 1795. By 1800, he was engaging in bizarre behavior. He was accused of being an incurable drunkard and hopelessly insane.

No one disputed his inability to serve as a judge, but under the Constitution, a federal judge could be removed only by impeachment. However, the Constitution specifically provided for impeachment for "treason, bribery, or other high crimes and misdemeanors." Drunkenness and insanity did not fit into any of those categories. Pickering was surely not guilty of bribery or treason—if he were in fact insane, he could not be guilty of committing *any* crime or misdemeanor under the common law.

This was not going to stand in the way of the Republicans, however. With Jefferson's encouragement, the Republican House voted articles of impeachment in March 1803. Pickering was convicted by the Senate the next year on a party-line vote. The message sent by this action was that the Republicans were willing to remove federal judges from office without regard for the actual language or the clear intent of the Constitution. This message must have reverberated among the members of the Federalist bench all the way to the Supreme Court.[10]

THE CASE

Among those positions created by the lame-duck Federalist Congress in the Judiciary Act of 1801 was that of justice of the peace for Washington County (in Maryland) within the District of Columbia. That position called for a term of office of five years. Unlike in modern days, in that era a justice of the peace held a position of great importance. It was the office that most impacted the day-to-day lives of the average citizen in the America of 1800. Justices of the peace then possessed executive, legislative, and judicial powers. Because they made up the legislature for the district's governance, they were like modern-day county commissioners. Justices of the peace also arrested and arraigned criminals and heard major civil cases. They held and advertised lost property and were responsible for assuring public morality. In sum, their duties were substantial, and the position carried with it a great deal of authority and influence within the local community.

When named as justice of the peace by President John Adams, William Marbury was thirty-eight years old. His father's family had once been wealthy but had lost much of that wealth. Marbury's grandfather had been a justice of the peace in Maryland before the family fell on hard times.

Marbury was a self-made man. He had aligned himself with the Federalist Party early on. Through contacts within that party, he had become agent for the state of Maryland and was commissioned to organize Maryland's chaotic finances. This position made him very powerful and quite wealthy. Later he was the agent of the naval yard in Washington, D.C. He became a member of the elite of Georgetown, joined the board of directors of the Bank of Columbia, and grew financially secure through investments and land speculation.

When the Federalist Party began to splinter into those who supported John Adams and those loyal to Alexander Hamilton, Marbury remained loyal to Adams. In return for this loyalty, Marbury was one of those men nominated by John Adams and confirmed by the Federalist Senate for justice of the peace in the District of Columbia. Marbury had reached the very peak of success not only in business but now in politics. But when his commission was not delivered by then-Secretary of State John Marshall before Jefferson was inaugurated, that position was snatched from him.

He was not going to give it up without a fight.[11]

Marbury hired Charles Lee, former Attorney General for the United States, and sued to obtain delivery of his commission from the new Secretary of State, James Madison. He filed his lawsuit directly with the Supreme Court, seeking a "writ of mandamus" from that Court. A writ of mandamus is an order from a court directing a public official to perform a specific act or to do a certain thing. In this case, Marbury wanted the Supreme Court to order the new Secretary of State to deliver the commission to him.

Marbury filed his action directly with the Supreme Court because the Judiciary Act of 1789 contained language that specifically allowed the Supreme Court to issue writs of mandamus. Such an action would have been the exercise of original jurisdiction, that is, something that the Court would hear argument on and decide as the court of first resort. (Original jurisdiction is in contrast to appellate jurisdiction, which is the authority of the Supreme Court to review the actions or the decisions of lower courts and decide whether or not those lower courts acted properly.)

Because the Supreme Court was hearing the case in the first instance, it had to conduct a trial. Witnesses were called and examined before the Court, and additional witnesses submitted affidavits or sworn statements in support of Marbury's case. Ironically, one of those witnesses was James Marshall, the brother of the Chief Justice, who had been acting as a courier for the State Department in the delivering of commissions.

The Supreme Court heard oral arguments and made its unanimous decision in February 1803.

In that decision, authored by Chief Justice John Marshall, the Court decided four questions. First, did Mr. Marbury have the legal right to the position of justice of the peace for Washington, D.C.? The Court said that indeed he did. It concluded that once the President had signed the commission, as John Adams had done, Marbury was entitled to the office.

The second question asked and answered by the Court was: If Marbury is entitled to the office, does he have a remedy under the law? This question was easily answered, for, as Chief Justice Marshall stated most emphatically, the government of the United States is a government of laws and not of men. If the United States were a nation of laws, there absolutely had to be a legal remedy to protect a legal right.

The third question asked and answered was this: If Mr. Marbury had a legal right to the position of justice of the peace, and since a legal remedy did exist, was that legal remedy a writ of mandamus issued by the Supreme Court of the United States ordering James Madison to deliver the commission? The answer to that question held a bit more peril for the Chief Justice.

As has already been described, the Supreme Court was a focal point of the contentious politics of its day. Jefferson had already concluded that the Federalist judiciary was a threat to his presidency and the Republican Party. In a private letter, he asserted the view, with some annoyance: "On their part, they have retired into the judiciary as a stronghold. There the remains of Federalism are to be preserved and fed from the Treasury, and from that battery, all the works of Republicanism are to be beaten down and erased."[12] If the Supreme Court asserted the right to tell Jefferson's executive branch officers what to do or not to do by way of the issuance of mandamus, Jefferson's fears would be realized.

The Court concluded that a writ of mandamus was in fact the correct legal remedy. Marshall made it clear, however, that the courts could not issue writs of mandamus in matters that were purely discretionary for executive branch participants. He said, "The Province of the court is, solely, to decide on the rights of individuals, not to enquire how the executive, or executive officers, perform duties in which they have a discretion."[13]

One can only imagine that as William Marbury read this opinion to this point, his hopes must have been high. He likely would have felt confident that he was indeed going to finally receive the position that the Republicans had deprived him of.

However, there was a fourth question that the Supreme Court had to decide, and that was whether it was for the Supreme Court to issue the writ of mandamus. To the chagrin of Mr. Marbury, the Court said no, and in doing so issued the judgment that a later Chief Justice of the Supreme Court said was "the most famous" decision ever issued by the United States Supreme Court.[14]

The unanimous Court concluded that in attempting to vest in the Supreme Court the power to issue a writ of mandamus, as Congress had done in the Judiciary Act of 1789, the Congress had acted unconstitutionally. It reasoned that Article III of the Constitution gives the Supreme Court original jurisdiction only in very specific cases: cases affecting foreign ambassadors and cases in which a state itself is a party.

Those are the only types of cases that can begin and end in the Supreme Court. The Supreme Court's remaining jurisdiction is appellate jurisdiction—that is, the right to hear and decide appeals from lower courts. Because the Constitution is so clear on the limitation of original jurisdiction, the Congress had violated the Constitution in attempting to expand the Court's original jurisdiction.

In reaching that conclusion, the Marshall opinion said something that is clear to us today, but that needed to be said with authority and precision in those early days of the new and untested American experiment in self-government. That something was that the Constitution was the fundamental and paramount law of the nation. The Congress could not change the Constitution by passing ordinary legislation. Because this was so, any law passed by the Congress and signed by the President that was in violation of the Constitution was void, invalid, of no force. The Constitution had to triumph over any normal legislative act of Congress or the President.

The Court was not done. In stating the preeminence of the Constitution over legislative and executive acts, the question arises: Who gets to decide when and whether such an act is in violation of the Constitution? To this the Marshall opinion said, "It is emphatically the province and duty of the judicial department to say what the law is."[15] It went on to state that if the Constitution and a law conflict with each other, the courts must decide between the two. The courts cannot close their eyes to the unconstitutionality of legislative acts. This was, in fact, "the very essence of judicial duty."[16]

Thus was born, to forever rule the American scene, the power of judicial review—that is, the United States Supreme Court is the final arbiter, the ultimate authority, the deciding voice, of constitutional questions.

DID THE FOUNDING FATHERS ANTICIPATE A SUPREME COURT THAT WOULD TRIUMPH OVER THE EXECUTIVE AND LEGISLATIVE BRANCHES?

History shows that the feared showdown between John Marshall and his cousin Thomas Jefferson was avoided. Marbury did not get his commission. He went on with his life. Further, the feared domination of the Republican Congress and Presidency by the Federalist judiciary did not materialize.

The ultimate conclusions of the Court, that the Constitution was paramount and that the courts got to decide whether and when a law violated that Constitution, were not terribly controversial. Since 1803, some have argued that John Marshall created a right for the Court that was never contemplated by the Founders—that the power of judicial review was made up out of thin air. Such is simply not true.

There is substantial evidence that this duty of the courts existed in the English common law system. At the Constitutional Convention it had been observed that the courts would have the right to void unconstitutional laws. This was, in fact, one of the selling points to those who feared the growth of national power and a potentially out-of-control Congress.

The best evidence that judicial review was contemplated by the Founders is to be found in *The Federalist #78,* in which Alexander Hamilton argued quite clearly that it would be the responsibility of the courts to reign in excessive and unconstitutional acts of the legislative branch. It was also pointed out that without such power in the courts, they would not be able to exercise the "check" required by the "checks and balance" system ingeniously envisioned by the Founders. There was also at least one Supreme Court decision prior to *Marbury* in which the Court had determined a separate Congressional act to be invalid.

Additional evidence that the *Marbury* decision was not exceptional is suggested by the reaction to that decision in 1803. The opinion received scant notice in the press. The case was reported on, but it was not criticized or characterized as earthshaking. Even Thomas Jefferson did not pay much attention to that part of the *Marbury* decision in which the Court declared that it is the duty of the Court to say what the law is. In the decades that followed, there were only a handful of critical comments made regarding the power assumed by the Supreme Court.

No, the authority of the courts to decide issues of constitutionality, now referred to as the power of judicial review, was not hotly debated in the decades after the *Marbury* decision. In part, that may be because the Supreme Court did not exercise its appointed power for over fifty years. The next time it found a legislative act to be unconstitutional was in the *Dred Scott* decision in 1857.

The issue that did generate heat was the question of whether the Supreme Court of the United States had that duty and power alone, or whether it was a duty and power shared with both the executive and legislative branches. Subsequent to the Court's decision, President Jefferson did not criticize his cousin's assertion of the power of judicial review. He simply asserted that the Supreme Court did not have the right to decide on the constitutionality of a matter for the President, just as the President did not have the right to decide on the constitutionality of a matter for the judiciary.

James Madison, often designated as the "Father of the Constitution," had argued before the House of Representatives in 1789 that though it was true the judiciary had the responsibility for clarification or interpretation of the Constitution, such power was not greater than that possessed by the other branches of the government.[17] Two of the most influential presidents in the decades following Jefferson, Andrew Jackson and Abraham Lincoln, generally shared Jefferson's view of the shared authority.

As good as the theory of shared responsibility may sound, it has no practical effect. It should be presumed that members of the legislative branch and the executive branch conscientiously consider the constitutionality of every piece of legislation that they vote on or sign. All the men and women who occupy those positions take an oath to support and defend the Constitution of the United States. Still, they pass legislation that courts find to be unconstitutional. That is also true of state legislators and governors. As a practical matter, although arguments are still made from time to time that the exercise of review of legislative acts is to be shared, those arguments have no effect or force. Such arguments are basically lost in history. It is a current reality that the ultimate authority on the Constitution of the United States is the Supreme Court of the United States and the Supreme Court alone. It is "supreme" in both name and clout.

It is important to note that John Marshall understood there to be limits to Court power of judicial review. In the *Marbury* opinion that he authored, the Chief Justice emphasized those limits: "Questions, in their nature political, or which are, by the constitution and laws, submitted to the executive, can never be made by this court."[18] It appears that one of the reasons that the power of judicial review was not exercised by the Supreme Court for over half a century was because members of that Court honored this view that they ought not to second-guess political and policy decisions made by the other two branches.

But restraint in this area was not to last. In the second exercise of judicial review, the 1857 *Dred Scott* decision, the Supreme Court waded fully into the political swamp. It declared unconstitutional an act of Congress, the Missouri Compromise of 1820. The Supreme Court also made the purely political decision that Americans of African descent could never be citizens of the United States and that the Congress had no authority to regulate the issue of slavery in the territories of the United States despite the Missouri Compromise of 1820.

Thereafter, the floodgates opened for courts to exercise judicial review in the last half of the nineteenth century. As noted, prior to 1860, the Supreme Court had ruled only two acts of Congress to be unconstitutional. Between 1865 and 1898, it held twenty-one acts of Congress to be in violation of the Constitution.[19] Not only did the Supreme Court exercise its authority more frequently, but the nature of the types of legislation it found to be unconstitutional became more and more controversial. The courts of the United States, both state and federal, exercised little restraint on the types of cases they would hear and the acts of legislative bodies that would be declared invalid and unconstitutional.

In the twenty-first century, the power of the Supreme Court to judicially review legislation passed by Congress and the states, and to declare that legislation unconstitutional, void, of no effect, and invalid, has become unchallenged.[20]

Every decision that will be analyzed and discussed hereafter is an example of the exercise of judicial review. Sometimes the Supreme Court voided state or federal legislation; sometimes it approved or endorsed state or federal legislation. In either type of case, the power of judicial review that is vested in the Supreme Court has shaped, molded, and reworked the United States of America.

NOTES

Epigraph: Rehnquist, *Supreme Court,* 35.

1. Forte, "Marbury's Travail," 350.
2. Library of Congress, "Religion and the Federal Government, Part 2."
3. For information about Washington, D.C., at the turn of the nineteenth century, see ushistory.org; EyeWitnesstoHistory, available at http://www.eyewitnesstohistory .com/pfcapital.htm.; Morison and Commager, *Growth,* 374–75; Rehnquist, *Supreme Court.*
4. Cunningham, *Pursuit,* 225.
5. For more information about the election of 1800, see Cunningham, *Pursuit;* Charles River Editors, *Election;* McCullough, *John Adams;* Wilentz, *Rise.*
6. For more information about the intention of the Founders regarding a federal judiciary, and the 1801 and 1802 Judiciary Acts, see Clinton, *Marbury v. Madison;* Madison, *Notes;* Nelson, *Marbury v. Madison.*
7. McCullough, *John Adams,* 560.
8. Supremecourthistory.org.
9. For more information about the biography of Chief Justice John Marshall, see Nelson, *Marbury v. Madison.*
10. See Rehnquist, *Grand Inquests,* 127–28; Adams, *History of the United States,* 143–45.
11. For more information about William Marbury, see Forte, "Marbury's Travail."
12. Rehnquist, *Supreme Court,* 28.
13. *Marbury v. Madison,* 1 Cranch 137, 170 (1803).
14. Rehnquist, *Supreme Court,* 35.
15. *Marbury v. Madison,* 177.

16. Ibid., 178. See generally *Marbury v. Madison;* Clinton, *Marbury v. Madison;* Nelson, *Marbury v. Madison;* Rehnquist, *Supreme Court.*
17. Spalding, *Founders' Almanac,* 199.
18. *Marbury v. Madison,* 170.
19. Nelson, *Marbury v. Madison,* 87.
20. For more information about the reaction to the *Marbury* decision and its aftermath, see Clinton, *Marbury v. Madison;* Nelson, *Marbury v. Madison.*

CHAPTER TWO

HOW THE SUPREME COURT CAME TO SANCTION RACISM

PLESSY V. FERGUSON (1896)

"This was the thesis, too, of the famous *Plessy v. Ferguson* decision of 1896 which, by accepting—or inventing—the doctrine of 'separate but equal accommodations,' threw the mantle of judicial approval over segregation."

—*The Growth of the American Republic*

I t was midway through a critical century in American history. The young attorneys were most anxious to take their case to trial. They wanted desperately to win a victory for their youthful client, a most sympathetic plaintiff—a five-year-old girl named Sarah Roberts. Every day, she had to walk a long distance up a great hill to attend her under-funded elementary school. In doing so, she had to pass five other elementary schools, all better financed and of a higher quality than hers. She had to walk so far past better schools for just one reason: she was black, and those schools were exclusively for white students.

When Sarah was just four years old, her father had obtained her admission into a school closer to her home, even though it was for white students. When the city's central school committee discovered that error, four-year-old Sarah was forcibly removed by police officers.

Young Sarah was represented by two attorneys, one black and the other white. The white attorney, Charles Sumner, was a fiery and passionate advocate for the rights of African-Americans. He and his partner, Robert Morris, argued zealously for Sarah, asserting that it was not right that she had to walk so far to attend an inferior school. They contended that being forced to do so traumatized the young girl and scarred her with feelings of inferiority.

Despite the best efforts of her attorneys, young Sarah was to lose her case. The court ruled that the local school officials had the authority to set school policy as they saw fit. Sarah had to continue her long daily trek to gain an education.

Was this a case brought somewhere in Alabama in 1950? South Carolina in 1953? Mississippi before the case of *Brown v. Board of Education?* No, it was Massachusetts, and the year was 1850. This was the first lawsuit ever brought to require integration of public schools in the United States of America.[1]

WE HAVE YET TO WIN THE QUEST FOR RACIAL HARMONY

Sadly, we live in a nation and at a time when race remains a major source of conflict and struggle. Daily headlines confirm the problem: allegations that white police officers are targeting young black men, frequent demonstrations to bring attention to racial disparities, demands for "safe places" for black students, racism as the cause of dissatisfaction with elected officials, the Black Lives Matter movement, and demands for social justice between the races. All these issues are conspicuously confronting citizens of the United States of America today.

Why? In light of such pioneering efforts as the early crusade of Charles Sumner in Massachusetts 160 years ago, the abolition movement that preceded the Civil War, the war itself that led to the freeing of approximately four million black Americans at the cost of hundreds of thousands of dead soldiers, and the passage of 150 years since the Civil War, why is it that we are still roiled with racial conflict?

How? How is it that a nation founded upon the splendid principle that "all men are created equal" cannot reach that goal? How is it that a nation that amended its fundamental document, the Constitution, to abolish slavery, guaranteed all the right to vote regardless of race, and secured equal protection under the laws for all—150 years ago—cannot find racial harmony today?

In order to better understand why our great nation has been unable to resolve the issue of race and has failed to establish complete harmony between our black and white citizens, it is necessary to understand what transpired in America in those critical years between the end of the American Civil War in 1865 and the dawn of the twentieth century. We need to look specifically at the year 1896, the year that the Supreme Court decided the critical case of *Plessy v. Ferguson*.

PRESIDENT ABRAHAM LINCOLN CALLS FOR ATONEMENT

It is 1865. Four million men, women, and children of African descent are now free. What is going to be the reaction of white Americans from both the North and the South to the plight of the freedmen? Are they going to welcome them into the mainstream of American life? Are they going to do everything necessary to atone for the great sin of slavery?

America's President, Abraham Lincoln, set forth a blueprint for the war-torn nation just weeks before the great fraternal conflict was to finally end—as was his life. In his Second Inaugural Address, delivered on March 4, 1865, Lincoln used carefully chosen words to inform the nation what he expected and hoped the American people would do as the Civil War drew to a conclusion. In that address, he made reference to the "one-eighth of the whole population" who were colored slaves. By choosing this language, he was reminding his audience that those who had been emancipated by Proclamation and military might were, truly, part and parcel with the population of the nation—they were not foreigners or a distinct, separate group.

Although he might have boasted of the great victory that was at hand and could have taunted the defeated South, he did not. Instead, he took but a gentle swipe at the Confederacy when, in referencing the North and the South, he quipped, "Both read the same Bible and pray to the same God, and each invokes His aid against the other. It may seem strange that any men should dare to ask a just God's assistance in wringing their bread from the sweat of other men's faces . . ." That was a stinging comment, but considering his immediate audience, it was actually quite mild. That audience would have included thousands who had lost loved ones—fathers, sons, husbands, cousins, uncles—in the four-year conflict. They deserved to be reminded that their loss was for a great cause.

In a demonstration of his greatness, the President then continued, "but let us judge not, that we be not judged."

He went on to assert that the entire nation was guilty of the sin of slavery and that the bloody conflict that was then drawing to a close was the result of that sin. "The Almighty has His own purposes. . . . If we shall suppose that American slavery is one of those offenses which, in the providence of God, must needs come . . . and that He gives to both North and South this terrible war as the woe due to those by whom the offense came . . . ?"

Continuing, he remarked:

> Fondly do we hope, fervently do we pray, that this mighty scourge of war may speedily pass away. Yet, if God wills that it continue until all the wealth piled by the bondsman's two hundred and fifty years of unrequited toil shall be sunk, and until every drop of blood drawn with the lash shall be paid by another drawn with the sword, as was said three thousand years ago, so still it must be said "the judgments of the Lord are true and righteous altogether."

And then, among the most gracious words ever spoken by a victor in war:

> With malice toward none, with charity for all, with firmness in the right as God gives us to see the right, let us strive on to finish the work we are in, to bind up the nation's wounds, to care for him who shall have borne the battle and for his widow and his orphan, to do all which may achieve and cherish a just and lasting peace among ourselves and with all nations.[2]

In proclaiming slavery to be a sin—a sin shared by the entire nation—President Lincoln was calling on the entire nation to atone for it. That atonement demanded justice for the former slaves. At a bare minimum, the former slaves must be guaranteed all the freedoms and protections afforded the white population of the United States.

Many responded to that call to guarantee justice, freedom, and protection. Among them was the lawyer in Sarah Roberts's lost cause of fifteen years before, Charles Sumner, now a member of the United States Senate from Massachusetts.

"THE PROSTRATE SOUTH"

The end of the American Civil War in April of 1865 found the defeated Southern states in most dire straits.

Millions of former slaves were now freedmen. Most were from rural areas and knew no other life than working plantations and farms. Many were uprooted and struggling for survival. The roads were filled with roaming men, women, and children. A large number found their way to cities and towns, hoping to find work. They lived in shantytowns, faced hunger, and were being fed by military units.

The South was exhausted and devastated. The damage to the landscape from battles and purposeful destruction was nearly universal. The economy was in shambles—in fact, there was no economy, with both agriculture and manufacturing all but gone.

Reconstruction was to come, but not overnight.

Looking back, it has been observed that the end of slavery altered the relationship between the white and black peoples of the South in a way that opened the door for the segregation that was to follow. In the "Old South," the South of pre-Civil War days, the interaction between the two races was considerable. Complete separation of the two races under slavery would not have worked:

> The very nature of the institution made separation of the races for the most part impracticable. The mere policing of slaves required that they be kept under more or less constant scrutiny, and so did the exaction of involuntary labor. The supervision, maintenance of order, and physical and medical care of slaves necessitated many contacts and encouraged a degree of intimacy between the races unequaled, and often held distasteful, in other parts of the country. The system imposed its own type of interracial contact, unwelcome as it might be on both sides.[3]

The interaction of whites and blacks was particularly true in the case of households, as claimed by African-American civil rights leader W.E.B. DuBois:

Before and directly after the [Civil] war, when all the best of the Negroes were domestic servants in the best of the white families, there were bonds of intimacy, affection, and sometimes blood relationship, between the races. They lived in the same home, shared in the family life, often attended the same church, and talked and conversed with each other.[4]

City dwellers, few though they were in the pre-Civil War South, also experienced an interaction that was not found in the North. It was common for whites and blacks to live in the cities side by side. There were no black ghettos in the South. That condition was found only in Northern cities.

This interaction and intimacy did not mean that the blacks were treated well. The interaction was for the convenience of the masters, but it did exist.

The end of slavery brought an end to this high degree of interaction and intimacy. The races were now at a distinct distance from each other. Much of the white population was on the verge of hysteria, and many feared that some of their former slaves might seek revenge. Civil authority had vanished. The army was in control, yet bands of marauders were common. In the immediate months after the war ended, the legislatures of many Southern states passed laws depriving the freedmen of their most basic civil rights. These laws were referred to, infamously, as "Black Codes." Such laws were not just the product of pure racism; they were in large part a reaction to the perilous conditions that existed in the South in the years following the Civil War.

It must be noted that racism and mistreatment of African-Americans was a sin not exclusive to the South, as Abraham Lincoln had forcefully asserted in his last major address to the nation. Even though slavery had been abolished in all of the Northern states by 1830, that did not mean that blacks were incorporated into the society and public life of those states. To the contrary, the common view of Northerners, even many of the most vocal enemies of slavery, was that "the Negroes were incapable of being assimilated politically, socially, or physically into white society.

They made sure in numerous ways that the Negro understood his 'place' and that he was severely confined to it."[5]

Ironically, whereas the interaction between the two races was consistent and frequent in the South before the Civil War, the North had segregated the black population—keeping its members in their proper "place." They were excluded from railroad cars and other means of public transportation. They were assigned their areas in theaters and restaurants. As already noted, they had their own schools. There were restricted areas of cities and towns where they were allowed to live.

Racism accompanied settlement of the West. In some new Western states, the state constitutions prohibited blacks from even entering the states' borders.

It was noted by some foreign visitors that the treatment of African-Americans in the North was harsher than in the South. For example, Alexis de Tocqueville wrote, "Racial prejudice appears to me stronger in the states that have abolished slavery than in those where slavery still exists; and nowhere is it shown to be as intolerant as in states where servitude has always been unknown."[6]

Blacks could not serve on juries in most Northern states before the Civil War. In five of the Western states they could not testify at a trial in which a white man was one of the parties. Only five of the Northern states, states that collectively were the residence of only six percent of the blacks who lived in Northern states, allowed blacks to vote. They were disenfranchised in all the other Northern states.

Abraham Lincoln reflected the views of most of the nation, North and South, when he stated in 1858, in the fourth of the Lincoln-Douglas debates:

> I will say then that I am not, nor ever have been, in favor of bringing about in any way the social and political equality of the white and black races, [applause]—that I am not nor ever have been in favor of making voters or jurors of negroes, nor of qualifying them to hold office, nor to intermarry with white people; and I will say in addition to this that there is a physical difference

between the white and black races which I believe will forever forbid the two races living together on terms of social and political equality. And inasmuch as they cannot so live, while they do remain together there must be the position of superior and inferior, and I as much as any other man am in favor of having the superior position assigned to the white race.[7]

It is arguable that the birth of segregation and the Jim Crow laws so infamously passed to ensure segregation took place in the North, not the South.

And, in truth, Abraham Lincoln knew of what he spoke when he attributed slavery and the mistreatment of African-Americans to the whole of the American nation.[8]

THE RADICAL REPUBLICANS AND CONGRESS, 1865–1875

Attorney-turned-Senator Charles Sumner was the leader of the group in Congress commonly referred to as the "Radical Republicans" in a Congress controlled by the Republicans. The Radical Republicans were a potent wing of the Republican Party. Members were distinguished by their hatred of slavery. During the Civil War they were openly critical of Abraham Lincoln, his conduct of the war, and his hesitation to free the slaves. After the war, they were slow to accept repentant Confederates, and they opposed the approach of President Lincoln's successor, Andrew Johnson, to Reconstruction of the South and his efforts to reunite the nation.

The Radical Republicans passed Reconstruction laws that imposed on the Southern states harsh terms to gain full reentry into the Union. Military governance was required until a former rebellious state had adopted a state constitution acceptable to the Radical Republicans. Normally, that meant a constitution that guaranteed the rights of blacks to vote and to hold public office. Another condition was that the state had to ratify the amendments to the Constitution of the United States that were forthcoming from the Radical Republicans in the Congress.

For, as significant as were the Reconstruction laws, they were only temporary. The Radical Republicans had higher aims and longer term objectives. It was their primary goal to reconstruct the entire nation to bring all black Americans into the mainstream of American life and to assure that they received their full measure of protection under the laws.

Charles Sumner led the Radical Republicans in the Senate. He had been elected to that body in 1851, and he used his position in the Senate to further his antislavery crusade. It frequently got him in trouble and once almost cost him his life. In 1856, he delivered a powerful speech against slavery, denouncing the "Slave Power" possessed by slave owners in the political arena. In the course of his two-day address, he condemned a member of the Senate from South Carolina, Andrew Butler, by name, accusing him of pimping for slavery. Two days later, Butler's cousin, Preston Brooks, a member of the House of Representatives, attacked Sumner on the Senate floor. With his cane he inflicted terrible wounds, leaving Sumner bloody and unconscious. Brooks ceased his assault only when his cane broke.

The episode polarized the nation. Brooks was hailed as a hero in the South, and Sumner was deemed to be a martyr in the North.

Sumner's injuries were severe enough that he did not heal quickly. He was not to return full-time to his Senate duties for three years. But he was not cowed by the attack. He immediately renewed his vociferous opposition to "Slave Power" and continued to do so while the Civil War unfolded. As soon as the war ended, Sumner—joined by the leader of the Radical Republicans in the House of Representatives, Thaddeus Stevens of Pennsylvania—forged ahead with a long-term agenda.

In short order, Congress passed the Thirteenth Amendment to the Constitution, which abolished slavery and involuntary servitude except in the case of punishment for a crime. This amendment was ratified by the states and became a part of the Constitution before the year of final victory, 1865, was to end.

The next year, Congress enacted the Civil Rights Act of 1866. That legislation guaranteed to all citizens, of every race and color, the same right to make and enforce contracts, to sue in court to protect those rights, to be a witness in court proceedings, to own and dispose of property, and to claim the right of protection of their property and their person under state laws. This last provision of the act was to assure that blacks were treated equally under the criminal laws of the various states. Often, the Black Codes provided for more severe punishment of a convicted black citizen than a white citizen for the exact same crime.

To eliminate any doubt that it had the authority to pass such a law, the Congress passed the Fourteenth Amendment to the Constitution and sent it to the states to be ratified. This amendment assured citizenship to the freedmen; prohibited the states from depriving anyone of life, liberty, or property without due process of law; and prohibited the states from denying any person equal protection of the laws and the "privileges and immunities" of citizenship. The Fourteenth Amendment was ratified by the states in 1868. The Southern states had to ratify this amendment in order to remove themselves from military governance.

The Radical Republicans knew that the right to vote was essential to protect the rights of the former slaves. To assure that the freedmen would never be disenfranchised, the last of the three "Civil War" or "Reconstruction" Amendments to the Constitution was ratified in 1870. It prohibited the federal government or the states from denying the right to vote to anyone based upon race, color, or previous condition of servitude.

Giving meaning to the words of the Fourteenth Amendment was the next—and was going to prove to be the last—of the major legislative achievements of the Radical Republicans. That effort took five years, from 1870 to 1875.

The culmination of the effort was the Civil Rights Act of 1875. That legislation banned racial discrimination in inns, theaters, common carriers (public means of transportation such as railroads and stagecoaches), and other places of public accommodation such as restaurants, parks, and places of amusement. As originally proposed, it also banned segregation in public schools.

Charles Sumner, consistent with the beliefs that had dictated his taking Sarah Roberts's case two decades earlier, was the primary advocate for the civil rights legislation in the Senate. He always insisted that the Civil Rights Act include a ban of segregation in the public schools. Between 1870 and his death in 1874, his single-mindedness made him a nuisance among his Senate colleagues. He was not popular or well liked, but his devotion to make the language from the Declaration of Independence, "all men are created equal," a reality in the lives of all Americans never wavered, nor was it ever doubted.

Critical to a discussion of the case of *Plessy v. Ferguson* that was to be decided twenty years later is an understanding of the lengthy debate over the concept of "separate but equal." Those who opposed the effort of Sumner and others to prohibit discrimination in public schools—and to a lesser extent the integration of inns, public transportation, and so on—attempted to amend the legislation to specifically allow for the separation of the races as long as the railroad cars, stagecoaches, inns, and schools were equal in quality and accessibility—in other words, separate but equal.

Perhaps the best argument against separate but equal schools was offered by a member of the House of Representatives from Wisconsin. He duly noted that it would inevitably foster prejudice, for it would result in "teaching our little boys that they are too good to sit with these men's children in the public school-room, thereby nurturing a prejudice they never knew, and preparing these classes for mutual hatred hereafter."[9] The same argument applied to any separate but equal facility.

Opposition to the Civil Rights Act was effective in delaying its passage for four years. It finally moved toward final passage in April of 1874. Before being passed by the Senate, that body rejected all efforts to include separate but equal language and to remove public schools from the legislation.

The House of Representatives gave the legislation much debate in the ensuing months. In the end, however, the legislation could not muster the required two-thirds of the members to overcome procedural roadblocks. It did, however, receive large majorities who approved of it with the Senate language prohibiting separate but equal facilities and including public schools.

But then came the fall elections.

The election of 1874 was a disaster for the Republican Party. The Democrats took control of the House of Representatives with a large majority.

In the lame-duck session before the transfer of leadership to the Democrats, the Radical Republicans in the House amended the Senate bill to remove its prohibition of segregated schools. Full integration of all other facilities and accommodations was commanded. Of great significance, an effort to amend the legislation to allow separate but equal facilities and accommodations was rejected by a wide margin.

The bill was then sent back to the Senate. It too was demoralized by the year's prior election, and it acceded to the removal of the language requiring integrated public schools. It passed the legislation, and President Ulysses S. Grant signed it on March 1, 1875.

Because it was passed within years of the Fourteenth Amendment, by a Congress that included many members who had been a part of the Congress that had passed the Fourteenth Amendment, the Civil Rights Act of 1875 is the most clear and accurate declaration of what it means for citizens of the United States to be entitled to equal protection under the laws of the states.[10]

Senator Charles Sumner had died in March of the previous year. He did not live to see the fruits of his lifelong effort to bring to all Americans the promise of the Declaration of Independence. His efforts were not in vain, however. Due to his commitment to true and universal equality, the Radical Republicans had put the highest elected body in the nation on record as being opposed to segregation in public venues and had specifically rejected the argument that separate but equal was an acceptable alternative.[11]

THE SOUTH IS GIVEN A CHOICE

In the immediate years after the Civil War ended in 1865, the two races in the South broke with their previous practice of interaction and forced intimacy. They became segregated in ways that they had not experienced before the war. However, that was not predestined to be a permanent condition. Soon, because of the Reconstruction Amendments, Reconstruction laws, and the Civil Rights Acts of 1866 and 1875, the two races began a period of contact, interaction, and relative harmony never before experienced. This period covered the years roughly from about 1875 to 1900.

In a book entitled *The Strange Career of Jim Crow,* by C. Vann Woodward, a book that Martin Luther King Jr. branded "the historical bible of the civil rights movement," Woodward described in detail this unique era:

> Black faces continued to appear at the back door, but they also began to appear in wholly unprecedented and unexpected places—in the jury box and on the judge's bench, in council chamber and legislative hall, at the polls and the market place. Neither of these contrasting types of contact, the old or the new, was stable or destined to endure for very long, but for a time old and new rubbed shoulders—and so did black and white—in a manner that differed significantly from Jim Crow of the future or slavery of the past.[12]

Many from both races were shocked to observe and then to experience blacks and whites eating together, working together, attending the same clubs and societies, and going to church together. They rode the same railroad cars and stagecoaches and steamboats. The integrated housing patterns of pre-war days continued.

Some specific examples of the historical record that Woodward collected are very enlightening:

A study in Virginia of the years between 1870 and 1900 found no demand on the part of the white population for supremacy, nor that blacks be disenfranchised. The two races rode in railroad cars and street-cars side by side. Sometimes blacks were excluded from eating places, but by no means was that the norm.

A number of visitors to the South in the period between 1870 and 1900 were surprised to find an absence of segregation and the existence of a reasonable degree of racial harmony.

One such visitor, Colonel Thomas Higginson, was a pre-war abo-litionist of an extreme stripe and the commander of a black regiment during the Civil War. His visit to Virginia, South Carolina, and Florida in 1878 shocked him. Characterizing himself as a "tolerably suspicious abolitionist," he looked for evidence of abuse of blacks but could not find it. He was pleased to find blacks exhibiting a degree of "manhood" and confidence that he had not seen in them previously. He compared the tolerance and acceptance of blacks in the South to that in the North in transportation, at the polling booth, in the courts and halls of the legis-lature, and on the police forces, and he found his native New England to be sorely wanting.

A visitor from England, a member of the British Parliament, trav-eled extensively through the South in 1879 specifically to observe racial practices. He wrote of his wonder at the degree of association and inter-face of the two races. His wonder included that the most humble black and proudest white could share a means of public transportation with no "malice or dislike on either side."

A South Carolinian wrote of the access of blacks to theaters, lectures, bars, and ice-cream saloons.

In 1885, an African-American newspaperman from Boston took a visit to his native South Carolina after being away for ten years. He left New York "with a chip on his shoulder" and dared anyone to knock it off. He was disappointed in that respect, for everywhere he traveled in the South he was met with acceptance, courtesy, and respect. He too compared his treatment with that of New England and found the South to be more hospitable. He sat at the same table with whites in restau-rants and was pleasantly surprised at the ease with which whites engaged him in conversation—much more ease than among whites in the North. Ultimately, he was to travel through Virginia, the Carolinas, Georgia, and Florida. After a few weeks, he cut back on his dispatches sent north because he had nothing exciting to write about.

Visitors from the North were often bothered by what they observed, the ease and frequency of interaction of the two races, including children at play, the proximity of homes in the cities, the friendliness of the maid and her mistress and the employer and his employee. They were surprised at the way a clerk treated a black customer in a store. Those visitors had not experienced it in the North and were not certain that they liked it.

Southern newspapers are a good source of information about this era and reasonably reflected the views of the broader society. As late as 1897, a Charleston, South Carolina, editorial strongly rejected the notion that South Carolina needed a Jim Crow system in transportation, for, among other reasons, it would be an "affront to our respectable and well behaved colored people."

An 1886 Virginia newspaper reported that no one in Virginia objected to attending political conventions with blacks, or serving on juries with blacks, or working with blacks.

African-Americans in the South were very active in the arena of politics. Their votes were sought by both political parties, and they were a powerful political force. Not only were they voters, but they were successful politicians. From 1869 until 1891, every session of the Virginia General Assembly had blacks as members. Between 1876 and 1894, North Carolina voters elected fifty-two blacks to their legislature, and in the 1870s to the 1890s, South Carolina elected forty-seven. In 1890, the state of Louisiana passed the Jim Crow law dealing with separate but equal railroad cars—the law that was to be considered by the Supreme Court in the *Plessy v. Ferguson* case. Sixteen blacks were members of that Louisiana legislature.

At the federal level, twenty blacks were elected to the Congress of the United States between 1865 and 1900; ten of them were elected after the end of Reconstruction. Every Congress between 1869 and 1901 had at least one black as a member.

The legislatures of the Southern states, usually under federal pressure, enacted legislation to protect their black populations. These legislative actions included those specifically mandated by federal law, for example, guarantees of the right to vote. But they went beyond that in many instances—for example, nearly all Southern states passed laws mandating equal access to transportation and other public accommodations.

The reasons for this era of relative harmony are numerous. To a degree it was a carryover of the pre-war norm. Much of it was driven by the Reconstruction laws and constitutional amendments and those state laws that sprang from them. Some of it was for pure political reasons— that is, to secure the political support of the black community. There was a code followed by many of the Southern elite that dictated their obligation to accept and assist the less fortunate, "inferior" blacks. Regardless of the motivation, this was a unique and relatively harmonious period in the South.

To be sure, not all was well in the Southern states in the last twenty-five years of the nineteenth century. There was violence, oppression, and subjugation of blacks. Voter suppression and mob violence occurred too often. But such affronts were more random than the norm. They were not systematic. They were not as pervasive and universal as they would later become.

As G. Vann Woodward concludes:

> My only purpose has been to indicate that things have not always been the same in the South. In a time when the Negroes formed a much larger proportion of the population than they did later, when slavery was a live memory in the minds of both races, and when the memory of the hardships and bitterness of Reconstruction was still fresh, the race policies accepted and pursued in the South were sometimes milder than they became later. The policies of proscription, segregation, and disenfranchisement that are often described as the immutable "folkways" of the

South, impervious alike to legislative reform and armed intervention, are of a more recent origin. The effort to justify them as a consequence of Reconstruction and a necessity of the times is embarrassed by the fact that they did not originate in those times. And the belief that they are immutable and unchangeable is not supported by history.[13]

Woodward, whose efforts to accurately account for the origin and expansion of Jim Crow laws and segregationist attitudes in the South is unparalleled, was stating an obvious point—that it was not inevitable that the South take the segregationist path. He demonstrated that even in the pre-Civil War era there had been interaction and intimacy between blacks and whites, and that such familiarity had expanded in the decades after the war. There was nothing in the culture of the South that demanded the system-wide racism of Jim Crow and segregation.

The South had experienced a degree of racial harmony, and thus it had perceived the alternative and always possessed a choice. Unfortunately for the history of our country and the lives of millions of African-American citizens, it chose the wrong and wicked path.

And, as will be shown, it was aided and abetted by the Supreme Court of the United States.[14]

THE EMERGENCE OF JIM CROW

The origin for the term "Jim Crow" is lost in history. An 1832 song using the name to refer to African-Americans is on record, but whether that was the first time the term was used is uncertain. Within a decade thereafter, its usage as a reference to blacks was common and has remained so since. Jim Crow laws are those that are directed at blacks, specifically those that demand segregation of blacks from whites.

Perhaps the first indication of the choice that the South was making, and the new direction to which it was committing, was in 1887 when Florida passed a Jim Crow law requiring segregation of all railroad facilities. Mississippi and Texas followed suit in the next two years.

As such laws began to sweep the South, voices of reason spoke out in resistance—in some instances in outright rebuke of the course being taken. As South Carolina was considering a Jim Crow law for railroads in 1898, the Charleston *News and Courier,* the oldest newspaper in the South, editorialized against the legislation: "As we have got on fairly well for a third of a century, including a long period of reconstruction, without such a measure, we can probably get on as well hereafter without it, and certainly so extreme a measure should not be adopted and enforced without added and urgent cause."

The editorial then went on to suggest the absurd yet logical outcome of taking this first step: "If there must be Jim Crow cars on the railroads, there should be Jim Crow cars on the street railways . . . passenger boats . . . waiting saloons at all stations . . . eating houses . . . jury box . . . dock and witness stand . . . Bible for colored witnesses to kiss . . . Jim Crow section in county auditors' and treasurers' offices. . . ."[15]

Sadly, nearly all of the absurd suggestions offered by the editor of the *News and Courier* were to become realities.

THE LOUISIANA EXPERIENCE

Louisiana, the state that gave us the *Plessy* case, is an excellent case study of the period of relative harmony and subsequent descent into Jim Crow that typified the South as a whole.

In 1868, the people of Louisiana adopted a constitution that was among the most progressive of the era. It provided for universal male suffrage. It required equal access and the privilege of usage to all places of a public character, meaning all places of public resort and every type of business or facility that required a license to operate. This included schools, streetcars, and all other public establishments. Race was prohibited as a consideration in the appointment to public office. These protections and integrative policies were not to be duplicated in scope until a century later.

The people of Louisiana elected large numbers of blacks to their state legislature—almost one-third of the members of the first Reconstruction

House of Representatives in the state were black. The state sent blacks to Congress. Louisiana had the first man of African-American descent to serve as its governor, P.B.S. Pinchback.

Much of the credit for Louisiana's efforts to bring African-Americans into the mainstream of the state's life was due to the large population of Afro-Creoles in and around New Orleans. Descendants of slaves and Europeans, primarily French and Spanish, this community was free, large, and very active in protecting its rights and those of all races.

These aggressive efforts at integration were not agreeable to some segments of the population of Louisiana. Because Louisiana was a model of integrationist success, the segregationists of Louisiana decided that they had to rely on extreme methods to dislodge the integrationists. Unlike most other Southern states, Louisiana (along with Mississippi and Georgia) experienced frequent and extreme instances of violence against blacks and the whites who supported them. An example was the massacre of both blacks and sympathetic whites at Colfax, Louisiana, in 1873. A confrontation arose between Democrat and Republican political supporters over the disputed gubernatorial election of 1872. There was a skirmish over control of the local county courthouse. It is estimated that more than fifty people were killed, and most of those were murdered after they had surrendered. The Colfax Massacre is one of the most deadly race clashes in our nation's history.

The widespread violence began to achieve its desired result. Blacks were browbeaten into surrendering their hard-fought-for rights. White supporters of integration were forced to abandon their black allies.

By 1890, Louisiana was ready to join the effort to eliminate the sharing of transportation facilities by blacks and whites. The state legislature passed a bill, the Separate Car Act, that required railroads in the state to provide separate but equal accommodations for whites and blacks. The railroad companies were legislatively mandated either to provide two separate cars or to divide one car in two so that whites and blacks would have separate accommodations. The intimacy that is the ordinary result of passengers riding in an enclosed railroad car, usually for long distances, was to be forbidden.

The Creole community of Louisiana had spearheaded opposition to the Separate Car Act. Its failure at the state legislature did not diminish its loathing of this piece of Jim Crow legislation—it hardened its resolve. The Creoles knew full well the slippery slope that their state had stepped onto, and they were intent on stopping the slide forthwith.

MANUFACTURING THE CASE OF *PLESSY V. FERGUSON*

A committee made up of prominent citizens, primarily French Creoles, was organized to challenge the 1890 Act. The "Committee of Citizens" included a former candidate for governor of Louisiana, a newspaper editor, a newspaper founder, and others active in the Louisiana civil rights movement.

A national appeal was made to raise money for a lawsuit, the Committee believing that the courts were its only hope for relief. Money was raised not only from the black community but from labor and civic organizations.

The Committee was able to enlist the services of one of America's most famous and committed civil rights attorneys, Albion W. Tourgée. A native of Ohio who had developed a hatred of slavery in his teenage years, he was to spend most of his life contending for the equal treatment of all. He was motivated by his religious belief that all men were God's creatures and that they should be treated equally and without prejudice. Like Charles Sumner, he was unbending in his views and cared little for the acceptance of those with whom he disagreed.

Tourgée had served with great distinction during the Civil War, suffering wounds that would trouble him the remainder of his life. Following the war, he and his wife moved to North Carolina to take advantage of the climate, which was friendlier to his health. In North Carolina he became a successful lawyer and judge.

Tourgée was a prolific writer, publishing fifteen political works of fiction and eight books of political and social analysis. He had a newspaper column that was published nationally. In that column he introduced the phrase "color-blind society," arguing that both society and the law had to be blind to color. His column was used to attack passage of the segregated railroad car laws that were becoming popular in Southern states. He had specifically called on the citizens of Louisiana to challenge its Separate Car Act in court. When asked, he agreed to serve the Committee's cause without compensation.

The Committee knew that a local attorney was required. They selected a man who had fought for the Confederacy, had success as an attorney and a judge, and was willing to take the case for $1000. His name was James Campbell Walker.

In their belief, the Committee had brought on board the very best legal team possible.

The Committee had its attorneys. Now they needed the perfect plaintiff. A twenty-nine-year-old shoemaker and repairman, Homer A. Plessy, was chosen. Plessy was born free. He had only one-eighth African blood. He had no appearance of being black, yet, under the Louisiana law, he was forbidden to ride in the railroad car designated for whites. His selection was calculated to focus the courts' attention, at least as a secondary issue, on the absurdity of racial classifications generally.

In a plot hatched with the railroad company (which objected to the Separate Car Act because of the costs imposed on it in providing separate but equal accommodations), Plessy bought a ticket and took his place in a white railroad car. The conductor had been apprised of Plessy's intended illegal action. According to the prearranged script, the conductor dutifully called on the railroad company's private detective to arrest Mr. Plessy.

A month later, Plessy appeared before Judge John Howard Ferguson. In 1892, the judge ruled that the Louisiana statute was constitutional because it was only intended to regulate rail travel within the state, and the state of Louisiana had that right. Mr. Plessy was found guilty. The state supreme court confirmed Judge Ferguson's decision.

The next logical step was an immediate appeal to the Supreme Court of the United States, but Tourgée delayed that step for as long as possible. In the end, that delay was to last four years, for Plessy's counsel desperately hoped for either a change in the makeup of the Supreme Court or a shift of public opinion against the tide of Jim Crow. After relying on various legal ploys, Tourgée finally ran out of delaying tactics, and in 1896 the case was called up before the Supreme Court of the United States.

It was easy to see why Tourgée had hoped for a new lineup on the Supreme Court.

THE SUPREME COURT AND ITS DECISION OF *PLESSY V. FERGUSON*

The Supreme Court of the United States had been no friend of the abolition movement before the Civil War, and it did not emerge from that bloody conflict as a friend of the civil rights movement afterwards. In 1857, it had ruled in *Dred Scott v. Sandford* that those of African-American descent could never be considered citizens of the United States. That radical interpretation of the Constitution of the United States was a direct cause of the Civil War.

In the *Slaughter-House Cases* of 1873, the first Supreme Court opinion to examine the Fourteenth Amendment, the Court gave an unexpectedly narrow meaning to the phrase "privileges or immunities" of the Fourteenth Amendment, holding that it only referred to the rights of citizenship bestowed by the federal government, not those rights of citizenship bestowed by the states. This narrow interpretation meant that the only rights protected by the language of the Fourteenth Amendment, which prohibited the states from abridging the "privileges and immunities" of its citizens, were the right to habeas corpus, interstate travel, and protection on the high seas.

A near-lethal blow to the civil rights movement occurred ten years later at the hand of the Supreme Court. In deciding five challenges to the Civil Rights Act of 1875, it declared the most important of its provisions unconstitutional in the decision known as the *Civil Rights Cases*. The essence of its ruling was that the Fourteenth Amendment was only intended to protect the citizens of the states against actions by the states, and could not dictate the actions of private parties. Thus, the efforts of Charles Sumner and the Radical Republicans to prohibit discrimination by the owners of railroads, innkeepers, and other individuals was declared to be beyond the reach of the Fourteenth Amendment. This decision simply disregarded the fact that many of the members of Congress who had written, debated, and passed that amendment also authored the Civil Rights Act of 1875. Surely they knew what the Fourteenth Amendment was intended to do, and that was what the 1875 legislation did.

Other cases not necessary to discuss here made clear to Tourgée and his clients that they would be facing an unfriendly Supreme Court. They also knew that the tide of public opinion was shifting dramatically against integration. This was true in the South with the emergence of Jim Crow laws in the arena of transportation. It was also a reflection of the long-held segregationist attitudes of the North.

In delaying the case for four years, Tourgée had urged a journalistic campaign to ignite opposition to Jim Crow, believing that it would put pressure on the Court to rule for Plessy. He had hoped for and believed in the goodness of the American people and in their desire to do the right thing. Tourgée had overestimated the American people, for no such public outcry was forthcoming.

In approaching argument to the Court, Tourgée enlisted the assistance of an old friend, Samuel F. Phillips. Phillips had been the United States Solicitor General who had argued the *Civil Rights Cases* before the Supreme Court. Between them, they believed they had a very good handle on the makeup of the Court. They realized that theirs was an uphill battle, but they held out hope. They analyzed with great care what arguments might be used to persuade those members who might be more pliable. They honestly thought that there were four Justices who would side with them, and they also believed that one of the other five might be persuaded by the right legal argument.

Just as they had underestimated the people of the United States, they underestimated the Supreme Court.

The Court issued its decision on May 18, 1896. Only eight of the nine Justices participated in the decision because Justice Brewer had not attended oral argument due to the death of his daughter. The Court found that the Louisiana Separate Car Act was not in violation of either the Thirteenth or the Fourteenth Amendments. The vote was seven to one, with only Justice John Marshall Harlan dissenting.

On the most important issue in the case, whether the Louisiana law that dictated separate but equal railroad cars was in violation of the Fourteenth Amendment, the Court found that it did not because they held that the act was a reasonable exercise of the state's police powers. From the beginning of our nation, it has been understood that the states have inherent powers to protect the health, safety, welfare, and morals of their people. These powers are referred to as the "police powers." The Court stated that this act separating the two races was a reasonable exercise of the police powers because it reflected the "established usages, customs and traditions of the people." This key finding was wrong in every respect.

It was wrong factually because the Jim Crow law in question was passed only two years before Homer Plessy boarded the train. The oldest such law was passed by Florida just three years before the Louisiana law. There was no basis for the Court to conclude that the practice of separating the races on railroad cars was an established custom, usage, or tradition.

The greatest error, however, was the fact that the Supreme Court totally ignored the impact of the Fourteenth Amendment on "established usages, customs and traditions." The very reason why the Fourteenth Amendment had become a part of the Constitution of the United States was to upend "established usages, customs and traditions."

As should be remembered from the discussion of the debates and votes leading to the passage of the Civil Rights Act of 1875, the act passed to incorporate into federal law the intention of the Fourteenth Amendment, Congress had overwhelmingly rejected the notion that separate but equal was acceptable in public transportation.

If the Supreme Court had relied upon the Originalist approach to Constitutional interpretation, it would have reached the conclusion that the state of Louisiana could not legally mandate separate but equal railroad facilities.

Instead, the Court interpreted the Constitution to reflect the emerging popular view of the nation, both North and South, that separation of the races was both desirable and necessary. In the four years between Homer Plessy's arrest and the Supreme Court's review of his conviction, laws similar to Louisiana's had become more commonplace. Such laws were being joined by others that outlawed interracial marriage. Because of intimidation and violence, fewer and fewer blacks were using the voting booth to protect themselves. Newly elected, all-white state legislatures were poised to unleash an avalanche of Jim Crow laws on the now-powerless black population throughout the South. The Supreme Court, in relying on the notion of "established usages, customs and traditions," was simply bowing to public opinion and the personal views of the members of the Court.

The dissenting Justice, John Harlan, proved to be the only Justice who recognized the import of the majority's decision. He speculated, as did the Charleston *News and Courier* two years later, on what was the logical extension of the majority opinion. He suggested that if a state could prohibit the two races from riding railroad cars together, why couldn't they compel the races to use different sides of the street, or prevent them from sharing streetcars, from sitting together in courtrooms, or from sitting together in the galleries of legislatures? Little did he realize that what he projected could be done, would be done before Jim Crow ran its full course.

In his dissenting opinion, Harlan adopted Tourgée's long-used phrase that the Constitution was intended to be color-blind, "and neither knows nor tolerates classes among citizens."

But the majority held that it was not to be.

Harlan drove one more verbal sword into the heart of the majority opinion when he asserted, "In my opinion, the judgment this day rendered will, in time, prove to be quite as pernicious as the decision made by this tribunal in the Dred Scott Case."[16]

Harlan proved to be correct. In what must be one of the most incredible ironies of modern history, a case that was intended to kill the practice of separate but equal in its infancy led to its transition into full adulthood overnight. As one scholar commenting on the case put it, "A case brought to chip away at Jim Crow instead added concrete foundation to it."[17]

Other scholars have gone so far as to suggest that the Jim Crow regime that followed was the "world of *Plessy*." That phrase is entirely accurate, for it was the Supreme Court of the United States that had undeniably endorsed and validated state-sanctioned discrimination.

DOES THE SUPREME COURT SIMPLY REFLECT PUBLIC OPINION AND THE VALUES OF THE PEOPLE IN ITS MOST FAR-REACHING DECISIONS?

In a real sense, the South arrived at a crossroads in the last years of the nineteenth century. It could have chosen to travel the path toward racial harmony, a path it had been traveling for twenty-five years. That course was not without its hazards and obstructions, but the South had proven itself capable of traveling it. Or, it could turn down the road toward the world of *Plessy* and Jim Crow.

Realistically, the Supreme Court could have erected a formidable if not insurmountable roadblock to movement down the path to Jim Crow. It did not—in fact, it effectively diverted the South down the Jim Crow path, and the South ran down that path with gusto.

What occurred thereafter is tragic in its scope.

Segregationists recognized that in order to implement their racial policies, they first had to eliminate the power of the blacks at the voting booth. Beginning with South Carolina in 1895, the Southern states began to pass laws to restrict black voting. These laws included literacy or property ownership tests for voting. Loopholes were incorporated into these laws to assure that white votes were not precluded.

It was not that no blacks owned property or that none were literate—but these tests were designed to provide hurdles that could be used by unscrupulous white officials to keep blacks from voting. Nefarious means were devised so that it became particularly difficult for a black landowner to prove property ownership. It became easy for an official to flunk a clearly literate black voter. It was just a strange coincidence that certain lists of property ownership or successful literacy test takers would be lost, or were discovered to be incomplete, at the polling place. White officials found other ways to manipulate the system to make it difficult, and in many cases impossible, for blacks to vote.

In addition, a poll tax was imposed in most of the Southern states. This tax was also designed to make it difficult for blacks to pay or, if payment *was* made, difficult to prove that payment at the time the vote was to be cast.

Where the tests and the poll tax failed, white segregationists fell back on violence and physical intimidation.

The combination of tests, taxes, and violence provided those intent on suppressing black voting a bundle of tools that proved to be very effective. For example, in 1896 there were over 130,000 registered black voters in Louisiana. Eight years later there were just over 1,300. In 1896 black voters had been in the majority in twenty-five parishes in that state, but by 1900 they were in the majority in none.

These instruments for disenfranchising blacks were challenged in the 1898 case of *Williams v. Mississippi.* The Supreme Court found no unconstitutional discrimination.

One of the side effects of the elimination of blacks from the voter rolls was their simultaneous elimination from jury duty. Most states selected potential jurors by relying on voting rolls. The elimination of blacks from voting rolls eliminated them from the list of eligible jurors.

Purging blacks from membership in the state legislatures eased the way for the passage of a myriad of Jim Crow laws. Until *Plessy,* the only laws that mandated the separation of the two races were in the area of transportation. In the next two decades, in many or most Southern states, laws were enacted at either the state level or by individual towns or cities mandating segregation in nearly every conceivable way.

Public education, which had never been integrated to any major extent, became firmly segregated.

The transportation venues covered by separate but equal laws or ordinances grew to include streetcars and steamboats. "Whites Only" and "Colored" signs showed up at theaters, inns, hospitals, mental hospitals, prisons, old folks' homes, orphanages, and homes for the deaf and blind.

In some states, blacks and whites were not allowed to work together in factories. Unions often excluded blacks from membership.

Public parks were segregated, as were circuses and other places of public amusement. In some cities, certain city blocks were designated for blacks, and no white family was allowed to live in that block. In turn, the remaining areas were off-limits to black families. In some small towns or cities, blacks were not allowed at all.

Water fountains and public bathrooms were segregated, as were telephone booths, textbooks, Bibles for witnesses at trials, and elevators.

In many states, no laws or local ordinances were passed requiring segregation in all of the specific instances just listed. Very often it just happened—it simply became the norm. The entire Southern existence was based upon segregation of the two races.

Whereas newspapers had once been effective supporters of the era of racial harmony, they now turned. Newspapers sensationalized stories of black crime, charges of rape, and examples of arrogance displayed by black citizens. This propaganda proved to be a catalyst that triggered a dramatic increase in violence against the African-American community.

Shamefully, many of the scientific journals and textbooks published during the heyday of Jim Crow included so-called "scientific evidence" of the inferiority of blacks and the superiority of the white race. Science was also relied upon to contend that there were irreversible mores to be found within each race that forever precluded their intermingling—the three last decades of the nineteenth century notwithstanding.

Within twenty years of 1900, blacks had disappeared from trains, streetcars, steamboats, the voting booth, public office, juries, judgeships, city councils, and Congress.

As the twentieth century unfolded, the North nearly caught up with the South in its downward path of the world of *Plessy*. Thousands of black soldiers returned home from military service in World War I expecting to be treated well for their sacrifice. They were not—anywhere. Tens of thousands of African-Americans migrated north to work in the emerging manufacturing sector. There, they were shoved into black ghettos. Lynchings occurred in both the North and the South, as did the emerging influence of the Ku Klux Klan. In 1919, race riots erupted in twenty-five cities scattered throughout the nation.

Jim Crow laws increased in the period of the 1920s and 1930s, applying segregation to barbershops, taxicabs, buses, and waiting rooms for interstate buses and airplanes. Segregation was demanded in baseball clubs, boxing matches, and racetracks.

By the 1940s, segregation was so universal that one observer remarked, "Segregation is now becoming so complete that the white Southerner practically never sees a Negro except as his servant and in other standardized and formalized caste situations."[18]

A caste system! That is what the world of *Plessy* created in the United States of America with the aid and assistance of the Supreme Court of the United States.

Our nation's history since 1950 reveals those agents of change that began to reverse our nation's caste system. Those agents of change included the military, civil rights organizations, Presidents, Congress, labor unions, and importantly the Supreme Court, when it determined that segregation of public schools was unconstitutional in the 1954 *Brown v. Board of Education* decision. But, over sixty years after *Brown,* we still do not experience peace in the area of relations between whites and black Americans.

WHAT IF?

Undoubtedly, *Plessy v. Ferguson* shaped the future of America in the area of race relations, not only in the decades that immediately followed its sanction of segregation, but today, 120 years following.

One cannot help but wonder how our history would have unfolded differently if the era of Jim Crow had not sapped the strength of the American character and culture as it did. Isn't it most likely that the indignity of slavery might have been more quickly and thoroughly purged from the consciousness of African-Americans?

In what ways might black Americans, thoroughly integrated into American society and culture for the entirety of the twentieth century, have made even more contributions in science, medicine, technology, the arts, and culture generally?

How might our economy have been stronger and economic growth enhanced if we had not artificially reduced the contributions to our economy of a major portion of our citizenry?

How might our nation's growth and prosperity have been boosted if we had increased the educational opportunities of all black children, instead of forcing them into separate and clearly unequal schools?

But for Jim Crow, it is likely that our nation would not have waited until the twenty-first century to elect its first African-American President.

How might the entire history of the twentieth century unfolded differently if the United States of America had been a bright symbol of racial equality and harmony to the entire world from the beginning of the century? Might our moral authority to encourage greater equality and justice to other nations have been enhanced if we were not living with the dark stain of Jim Crow?

Although it will always be mere speculation, it is not unreasonable to believe that had America never entered the world of *Plessy* and Jim Crow—an era that harmed at least three generations of Americans, both blacks and whites—the current discontent and division in American racial relations might be very different.

NOTES

Epigraph: Morison and Commager, *Growth of the American Republic*, 88.

1. For more information about the case of Sarah Roberts, see Kendrick and Kendrick, *Sarah's Long Walk*.
2. Second Inaugural Address of Abraham Lincoln, available at avalon.law.yale.edu.
3. Woodward, *Jim Crow*, 12.
4. Ibid.
5. Ibid., 18.
6. De Tocqueville, *Democracy*, 329.
7. Found at http://teachingamericanhistory.org/library/document/the-lincoln -douglas-debates-4th-debate-part-i/.
8. For information about the condition of African-Americans in both the North and the South, see Woodward, *Jim Crow*.
9. McConnell, *Originalism*, 1014.
10. For a full discussion of the efforts by Congress to assure protection of the recently freed African-Americans, see McConnell, *Originalism*.
11. For more information about the life of Charles Sumner, see Donald, *Charles Sumner*.
12. Woodward, *Jim Crow*, 26.
13. Ibid., 65.
14. Woodward's account of the history of Jim Crow legislation and attitudes is in contrast to the generally accepted historical narrative. Most histories seem to ignore the evidence that Woodward compiled, apparently because it does not fit the popular mold of implacable racism among the white population of the South. However, Woodward was too much of a scholar and his work was accepted by too many historians to not be given its due as an accurate representation of the evolution of Jim Crow and segregation.
15. Woodward, *Jim Crow*, 67–68.
16. *Plessy v. Ferguson,* 163 U.S. 537 (1896). For more information about the *Plessy* decision, see Elliott, *Color-Blind Justice;* Hoffer, *Plessy v. Ferguson;* McConnell, *Originalism;* Morison and Commager, *Growth of the American Republic;* Thomas, *Plessy v. Ferguson;* Woodward, *Jim Crow.*
17. Hoffer, *Plessy v. Ferguson,* 3.
18. Woodward, *Jim Crow,* 118.

CHAPTER THREE

HOW A LAW ON BAKERS' WORKING HOURS LED TO ABORTION RIGHTS

LOCHNER V. THE STATE OF NEW YORK (1905)

"To this day, when a judge simply makes up the Constitution he is said 'to Lochnerize.'"

—*Judge Robert Bork*

From time to time, the Supreme Court of the United States makes decisions that are polarizing. No decision fits that description more aptly than the 1973 decision of the United States Supreme Court in *Roe v. Wade.* Few Supreme Court opinions are better known and none is responsible for generating more genuine heat than *Roe*—even though more than forty years have passed since the case was handed down.

Only a handful of people do not know what the *Roe* case was about— the desire of Jane Roe, real name Norma McCorvey, to overturn existing abortion laws. Hardly any know, however, that the Supreme Court's decision in *Roe v. Wade* was made possible because of the way the Supreme Court decided a case involving a dispute over the working hours of bread bakers in New York seventy years before.

POLICE POWER: THE AUTHORITY OF STATES TO LEGISLATE AND REGULATE

By what authority do states tell us what to do? State legislatures commonly pass legislation regulating businesses large and small, as well as the public and even the private behavior of individuals. This includes telling us everything from what we must pay our employees to how fast we can drive our vehicles to what we can eat and drink.

By what power do they do so? The answer is commonly referred to as the "police power." This is the term that has traditionally been used to describe the power of states to legislate and to regulate. It is inherent in the American theory of government—that theory by which the people create governments and surrender certain rights to them in order for those governments to carry out the responsibility of protecting the bulk of our God-given rights of life, liberty, and the pursuit of happiness.

A state carries out that responsibility, and in doing so employs its police power, when it passes laws to protect the health, safety, welfare, and morality of its citizens. For example, laws that prohibit prostitution are passed to protect the community's health and morals; laws that require minimum safety standards at the workplace are to protect the safety of its citizens; zoning laws are authorized by the police power to protect the welfare—in this case, the property—of its citizens. Laws requiring children to be immunized promote health. Most criminal laws are based upon the state's obligation to protect the health, safety, welfare, and morality of its citizens. The possible examples of the exercise of the police power are nearly endless.

In our system of government, the police power that the states can exercise is protected by the Tenth Amendment to our Constitution. That amendment, which was part of the Bill of Rights, says, "The powers not delegated to the United States by the Constitution, nor prohibited by it to the States, are reserved to the States respectively, or to the people."

It is obvious that every time a state exercises the police power, the liberty or freedom of the people is constrained in some way—great or small. In each instance of the state exercising its police power, we are told that we have to do something or we are prevented from doing something. The critical question then becomes: What limits the state's police power?

It was understood by those who founded this nation that the first and foremost way by which limitations or boundaries would be fixed on state legislatures would be through the ballot box—that is, what the voters would tolerate. Whenever state legislatures pass laws that are unacceptable to the majority of the voters, it is expected that an activist citizenry will seek a new legislature to correct that error.

The second limitation on the exercise of the police power is what the constitutions of the respective states and the Constitution of the United States will permit. The police power cannot infringe on rights guaranteed or protected by state constitutions or the Constitution of our nation.

In the previous chapter we learned that the state of Louisiana was relying on its police power in ordering railroads to provide separate but equal railroad cars. The Supreme Court decided in *Plessy* that Louisiana's exercise of its powers did not conflict with the Fourteenth Amendment to the Constitution, and thus Louisiana was allowed to proceed to segregate. The case of *Lochner v. The State of New York* was decided just a few years later, but the Court's conclusion regarding legislation passed by the state of New York to protect the bakers of bread was very different.

THE ERA

At the turn of the twentieth century, as the American people took stock of the changes that had come about in the first one hundred years of the nation's existence, they had much to look to with pride. There was no more frontier to conquer—western expansion was complete. The population of the United States had grown from five million to seventy-six million. The Constitution had proven extraordinarily resilient—surviving foreign wars, depressions, a great Civil War, corrupt governments, the western expansion, and prosperity. America was now among the richest nations on earth, and some believed that the average American was better off than any other people on earth. The opening of educational opportunities for the common citizen, advances in the sciences, miraculous inventions, increased agricultural productivity, and growth in the arts and culture placed the United States of America at the top of the nations of the world.

But these successes had not come without significant costs.

The land had been conquered, but in that conquering, the land, water, and woodland had been abused. America was a major participant in, and beneficiary of, the Industrial Revolution that shook the world in the last half of the nineteenth century. But the wealth that had been generated by that revolution came at the price of abused workers, including children and women. Industrial injuries and deaths were common. Wealth was being amassed in the hands of a few. Unregulated trusts and monopolies in manufacturing and major industries were common.

In addition to America being industrialized, it was also being urbanized. The result was slum living, where dirt, crime, disease, and corruption were rampant. Many politicians were crooked, and political "bosses" and kingpins were common. Little was being done for the aged, the infirm, the orphan, or the unhealthy. Many still suffered from hunger and inadequate housing.

Beginning in about 1890, the United States entered into what has since been labeled the Progressive Era—that period when the nation began to face up to its failings and shortcomings. Government became more active in solving the nation's ills. Legislation to break up trusts and monopolies was passed at the federal and state levels. Political reform struck at the corrupt and the bosses.

Labor unions became a force to be reckoned with. Regulation of business and industry by the states to address worker welfare became common. The case of Joseph Lochner, small-time New York baker, is a tale about those efforts in the state of New York.[1]

Urbanization and industrialization had a distinct impact on the baking business. Baked goods, especially bread, were a staple of the American diet. As more women moved into the workforce, there were fewer who had the time to bake. Furthermore, as Americans relocated to the cities, most found themselves living in high-rise, apartment-type dwellings known as tenements. These were small, cramped apartments that often had several families sharing limited space. Few of these tenements had adequate cooking facilities, and the women rarely found themselves with stoves to bake in. The result was an explosion in the demand for commercial baked goods, bread in particular. In the last fifty years of the nineteenth century, that period characterized by urbanization and industrialization, the number of those employed in the baking industry grew almost tenfold.

In the crowded tenements of the growing cities, bakeries sprang up in the basements of tenement buildings. These were typically small businesses with only a handful of employees. The convenience of being close to their customers kept the cost of transporting bread and other baked goods to a minimum. The cellars of tenement buildings were cheap to rent, largely because they were dark, dirty, and otherwise useless space for the owners of the tenements. Clay or brick sewer lines shared the same space with the bakeries. There were no vents for fumes or dust. Usually the floors were dirt.

Not only were the accommodations unsafe and unsanitary, but the baking process did not lend itself to cleanliness or safe working conditions for the employees. Bathroom facilities were lacking and thus hands did not get washed. The bakers were not particular about personal hygiene generally. Often the bakeries served as the sleeping quarters for the employees. The combination of no ventilation, heat and cold, flour dust, and gas fumes from ovens resulted in high rates of what was then referred to as consumption, lung diseases of various origins.

Baking was hard work. Employees had to lug heavy sacks of flour and dough. Reports of huge globs of dough being hauled around the cellar bakery on the hip of a dirty, sweaty baker were not unknown.

Most employees of these small businesses were recent immigrants to the United States. They were willing to work for low wages, and the owners obliged them.

But as awful as was the pay, the biggest complaint of the bakers was the hours they were required to work. A normal work week for a baker in 1895 was seventy-four hours, consisting of six twelve-hour days plus a couple of hours tacked on somewhere. Many bakers worked even longer hours. One state inspector found a bakery that required its workers to work six days for fifteen hours per day plus a twenty-four hour shift on Thursday, for a total work week of 114 hours.

The hours were so long that it was impossible to have a normal family life. Most of the bakers worked from early evening until the next morning or early afternoon, so seeking opportunities for education or vocational training was nearly impossible. There was no time for lectures or museum visits. There was no time for recreation and relaxation.

The combination of unhealthy working conditions, low wages, and long hours made the life of a baker quite miserable. Yet there was never a shortage of workers willing to do the work.

The labor movement that took root and grew after the American

Civil War made a shorter working day its priority—even above demands for better wages. The battle for fair wages was one that had to be fought industry by industry, if not employer by employer. On the other hand, the "eight-hour movement" was focused on government solutions.

Eight-hour advocates made high-sounding arguments for their program's implementation. Family life would benefit from an eight-hour working day. Better citizens would result from having more time during the evening to participate in public affairs, cultural events, and such. It was argued that a more educated and informed employee would benefit not only employers but also the community at large.

It was also argued that legislation requiring eight-hour workdays would increase employment opportunities—for surely the employer would want his production to remain the same, and that would require the boss to hire more employees to fill the newly vacated hours. It became the accepted economic theory that the more people who were employed, the more customers with money there would be, which in turn would increase the demand for manufactured goods, and such increases would result in an even greater need for employees.

The first targets for legislation limiting working hours were women and children. In 1874, Massachusetts became the first state to limit their working day to ten hours. Other states followed suit. Government employees were also legislated into shorter workdays. Specific hazardous jobs were also targeted for reasonable workdays, including miners, railroad workers, and smelter workers.

Some labor leaders hesitated to seek relief, even for a shorter workday, at state legislatures. They held to the belief that bargaining with business and employers directly was the most effective route to success. Some union leaders feared they would lose their power over their union members if the members saw legislatures rather than the labor bosses as their champions.

One union leader who was not of that mind was the head of the Bakers and Confectioners' International Union of America, Henry Weismann. A German-born baker by trade, he had come to America, dabbled as an anarchist in California, and then moved to New York, where he clawed his way to the top of the bakers union. He was not afraid of seeking legislative remedies for his baker members, especially since the number of small business bakeries was beyond the capacity of any organization to bargain with one at a time.

In the mid-1890s, an opportunity arose in the state of New York for a legislative fix to both the unsavory working conditions and the untenable working hours of small, tenement-cellar bakers. A state legislative committee looked hard at the overall problems of tenement living. Overcrowding, high mortality rates, disease, safety issues generally, and the absence of proper sanitary facilities, parks, and playgrounds were the focus of the committee's investigation.

Among the committee's findings was the discovery that cellar bakeries were the source of an inordinate number of fires in tenement buildings. This finding on basement bakeries prompted one member of the committee, a reporter and editor for a New York newspaper, to undertake additional investigatory work on his own. His published exposé stunned the state. He reported on the unsanitary and unhealthy conditions to be found in the cellar bakeries and thereby raised doubts as to the healthiness of the products they produced. He also included in his stories accounts of the miserable working conditions and dreadful demands put on bakers.

With these widely published stories on the minds of the citizenry, Henry Weismann jumped into the fray. A sponsor for a piece of legislation was found and a bill was introduced in February 1895. The New York Bakeshop Act was passed by the New York legislature by a vote of 90 to 0 in the State Assembly and 29 to 0 in the State Senate; it was signed by the governor in May 1895.

The Bakeshop Act demanded sanitary baking methods and a healthy working environment for the employees. Prominent among the requirements of the Bakeshop Act was language that read, "No person shall be required, permitted, or suffered to work in a biscuit, bread or cake bakery more than sixty hours in one week, or more than ten hours in one day."

This was an absolute prohibition. There was no loophole for the payment of overtime pay when hours in excess of ten in one day were worked. Further, a violation was a crime. To ensure that there were teeth to the new law, state inspectors were hired to monitor compliance with it.

The stage was set for Joseph Lochner, the owner of a small bakery in Utica, New York, to make his stand.

THE CASE

When the Bakeshop Act was being debated and passed by the New York legislature, there was little organized opposition. That accounts for the unanimous votes in favor of the legislation. However, once the effects of the legislation became apparent, specifically the ten-hour rule, the bakers of the state became agitated. They organized, and the New York Master Bakers Association came into being. This association represented primarily the small bakers of the state. The large, unionized bakers had little problem with the ten-hour rule because they had plenty of employees to take over at the end of a ten-hour day. They were also capable of paying overtime if it was necessary. Neither was true for the small bakers.

The Master Bakers Association did not oppose the health and safety requirements of the Bakeshop Act, but they were adamantly opposed to the ten-hour provision. One of the reasons was that there were certain occasions when overtime work in a small bakery was simply required— Thanksgiving and Christmas Days being prime examples. When those times came, the bakers did what they had to do, and that was to violate the law. This opened the door to labor union blackmail. The union knew that bakers had to have their employees work for more than ten hours on certain days; in fact, they often negotiated labor agreements with bakers that allowed for employees to work more than ten hours in a day— if overtime pay was paid. In most cases, however, to pressure bakers to sign favorable contracts, the labor union would threaten bakers that they would report violators. The labor union also pressured state inspectors to prosecute if the baker did not surrender to the generous terms demanded by the union.

Henry Weismann, the labor leader who had led the effort to pass the Bakeshop Act, came to see how the act was being abused. He began to publicly bemoan the use of the act as a primary tool of blackmail. It was the first step Weismann was to take to distance himself from his roots as a labor partisan. It was not to be his last.

The Master Bakers Association decided they had to challenge the ten-hour law. They looked for a good test case and settled on Joseph Lochner as the defendant.

Lochner was a German immigrant. He had learned the baking trade in Utica, New York, and had opened his own bakery there in 1890. Originally, he operated a union bakery. But when he had the audacity to allow one of his young employees, Aman Schmitter, to live with him, trouble followed.

Schmitter did not want to live with his family, nor did he want to live alone, so Lochner took him in. Unfortunately for Schmitter, Lochner's union contract did not permit an employee to live with his employer. Schmitter appealed to the union but was rebuffed. Disgusted, Lochner chose to deunionize rather than put Schmitter out on the street. The union attempted to boycott Lochner, but it failed. It did, however, succeed in making Lochner despise unions.

Thereafter, he repeatedly rejected efforts to reunionize his small bakery. The union responded by reporting him to the state inspector when he violated the Bakeshop Act by allowing an employee to work more than ten hours while learning the art of cake making. He was prosecuted and fined twenty dollars.

A few years later, Lochner was again in trouble. To all appearances, he was the victim of a labor union informer. He was accused of allowing Aman Schmitter to work for more than ten hours in one day. In light of the history between Lochner and Schmitter, including the fact that Schmitter was to work for Lochner for many years thereafter, it was more likely that the prosecution was initiated by Lochner himself, or the Master Bakers Association of which Lochner was a member. Regardless, this time he was to become the test case to determine the constitutionality of the Bakeshop Act ten-hour provision.

At trial, Lochner refused to plead either guilty or innocent. He was a hardheaded man! The trial judge had no choice but to find him guilty and fined him fifty dollars.

The case was appealed through the state court system of New York, and eventually it went to the Supreme Court of the United States. His appeal was to be argued before the Supreme Court by none other than Henry Weismann, who had resigned his position with the labor union, graduated from law school, and now came to the aid of the Master Bakers Association and Joseph Lochner.

THE OUTCOME

Scottish economist Adam Smith, famous for his book *The Wealth of Nations,* asserted in that book:

> The property which every man has in his own labour, as it is the original foundation of all other property, so it is the most sacred and inviolable. The patrimony of a poor man lies in the strength and dexterity of his hands; and to hinder him from employing this strength and dexterity in what manner he thinks proper, without injury to his neighbor, is a plain violation of this most sacred property. It is a manifest encroachment upon the just liberty, both of the workman, and of those who might be disposed to employ him.[2]

Adam Smith simply stated what is obvious to most of us—the birthright of all is the right to work as long and as hard as we wish. That right to work is a form of property owned by the individual. To arbitrarily infringe on that right is stealing that birthright or property from that individual. To prevent people from working not only deprives them of their property, it also infringes upon their liberty—and not only their liberty, but the liberty of the one who wants to employ them. This is what the Bakeshop Act did when it prohibited Aman Schmitter from working more than ten hours in one day. It also deprived Joseph Lochner of his liberty to work his employees for as long as they wanted to work.

That quote from one of the most esteemed economists and philosophers of all time quite likely summed up Joseph Lochner's instinctive reaction to the New York Bakeshop Act.

At the time Joseph Lochner was pursuing his case to the Supreme Court, the concept that an employee had the right to enter into a contract with an employer to work as many hours as they could agree upon was not yet established. True, in 1897, the Supreme Court had referred to a "liberty of contract"—the notion that the term "liberty" included the right for individuals to enter into contracts free of state intervention. That case, however, had to do with the freedom to enter into insurance policies, hardly a good precedent for Joseph Lochner's case.[3]

The notion that, in exercising their police powers, states could interfere with the right of employers and employees to contract for whatever hours and wages they might agree upon had been before the Supreme Court before. In a case involving a Utah law that limited the hours that miners could work to just eight each day, the state law had been deemed constitutional by the Court.[4] In another decision, issued just two years before it took up Joseph Lochner's case, the Supreme Court had upheld a state statute that limited state employees and employees of state contractors to eight-hour days.[5] In other cases involving state labor legislation, the Supreme Court had proven to be hesitant to overturn such laws.

The law and precedent were not on Mr. Lochner's side.

But that did not discourage the determined Mr. Lochner or his attorney, Henry Weismann. They argued the case before the Supreme Court in February of 1905, and the Court rendered its opinion in April. Surprisingly, Joseph Lochner won, with the Supreme Court split 5–4.[6]

In order to understand the majority opinion in *Lochner,* one must understand the concept of "due process" and how its meaning had morphed in the decades before *Lochner.*

If you were to ask Everyday Person what "due process" means, he or she would probably say something like, "There have to be rules in place, and the government has to play by those rules." That pretty accurately sums up the notion.

The concept originated in the Magna Carta of 1215. The specific phrase "due process of the law" was first used in an amended version of the Magna Carta in 1354. Clause 29 of that most famous of English documents said that no man could be put out of his property, nor disinherited, nor put to death without "due process of law."[7]

One of the original amendments to the Constitution of the United States, the Fifth Amendment, states that no person can be deprived of life, liberty, or property without due process of law. For the first seventy-seven years of our nation's life, that language limited the power of the federal government against its citizens. The Fourteenth Amendment, added to the Constitution in 1868, extended the limitation to the states. That amendment contains the language that "nor shall any State deprive any person of life, liberty, or property, without due process of law." By that language, the citizens of the United States gained protection against arbitrary state action.

The term *due process* was understood from the beginning—from 1215 going forward—to mean that the government could not punish its citizens, whether it be taking their life or liberty or property, without following the rules. Those rules were understood to include giving the citizen a fair opportunity to be heard. Those rules meant that regular procedures had to be followed. Governments could not act arbitrarily or abusively. In the context of the passing of legislation, it meant that laws would be passed according to constitutional requirements.

Due process was understood to refer only to the *means* by which life, liberty, or property is taken from a citizen. In the realm of legislation, it had nothing to do with the substance or content of the legislation—only the *means* by which the law or legislation came about.

But beginning with the infamous *Dred Scott* case of 1856, courts in the United States began to pollute the simple meaning of *due process* to give it a substantive meaning. That is, courts began to say that the due process language of the Fifth and Fourteenth Amendments put limits on the *substance* of the legislation—what the legislation did, what it said, what liberty rights it affected—not just the procedure by which it came about. This became known as *substantive due process*.

By this development, the courts assumed the role of deciding whether certain state laws, passed in reliance on the police powers that the states possessed, were in fact unconstitutional because they infringed on the "liberty" interest protected by the Fourteenth Amendment. The courts took upon themselves the power to define what the term *liberty* means.

This was an enormous power that they assumed.

That power was exercised in Joseph Lochner's favor.

In his case, the majority opinion stated that the New York Bakeshop Act "interferes with the right of contract between the employer and employees, concerning the number of hours in which the latter may labor in the bakery of the employer. The general right to make a contract in relation to his business is part of the liberty of the individual protected by the Fourteenth Amendment to the Federal Constitution. Under that provision no state can deprive any person of life, liberty, or property without due process of law."[8]

Later in the opinion, the Court asks the question, "Is this a fair, reasonable, and appropriate exercise of the police power of the state, or is it an unreasonable, unnecessary, and arbitrary interference with the right of the individual to his personal liberty . . . ?" And in answer to that question, the Court concluded, "There is no reasonable ground for interfering with the liberty of person or the right of free contract, by determining the hours of labor, in the occupation of a baker."[9]

Ironically, in the intervening paragraph, the Court said that it was not for it to substitute its judgment for that of the legislature—but that was just what it was doing. It mattered not to the Court that the New York Bakeshop Act had been passed by the legislature of New York without a single "no" vote.

By those conclusions, the Supreme Court of the United States established three precedents—and in the process greatly inflated the Court's power.

It first affirmed that *due process* does not just mean *process*, the means by which legislation comes about—no, *due process* also means what the legislation says or does, what the law's substance is. One commentator suggested that the Court's redefining the word *process* was akin to what Humpty Dumpty does in response to Alice in *Through the Looking Glass* when he proclaims, "When I use a word, it means just what I choose it to mean—neither more nor less."[10] The phrase *substantive due process,* which has been used to describe the legal doctrine given birth in *Lochner,* has duly been noted to be a contradiction in terms, once characterized as being similar to describing something as "green pastel redness."[11]

Second, it affirmed that courts possess the power to define the term *liberty* when that term is used in the due process clauses of the Constitution of the United States. Stated another way, the courts are the final arbiter of what rights are included in the term *liberty.* In Joseph Lochner's case, liberty included the heretofore unknown right to contract for one's labor, a right nowhere stated or even alluded to in the Constitution.

Third, it made itself the ultimate decider as to whether or not any legislation of a state legislature "unreasonably" interfered with that liberty interest or right—and if it did, the courts possess the power to declare the law unconstitutional and void.

This is the sum and substance of what substantive due process is—the power to define *liberty* as five members of the Supreme Court think it should be defined, and to then decide whether a state's infringement of that liberty is "reasonable" or not.

Lochner was the field upon which the Supreme Court of the United States successfully made a great power play.

Substantive due process thus became and remains a primary source of the Supreme Court's ability to shape America as it sees fit. A subsequent member of the Supreme Court, Hugo Black, concluded sixty-five years later that:

The many decisions of this Court that have found in that phrase [due process of law] a blanket authority to govern the country according to the views of at least five members of this institution have ignored the essential meaning of the very words they invoke. When this Court assumes for itself the power to declare any law—state or federal—unconstitutional because it offends the majority's own views of what is fundamental and decent in our society, our Nation ceases to be governed according to the "law of the land," and instead becomes one governed ultimately by the "law of the judges."[12]

A former judge of the United States, and one of our nation's greatest legal minds, has said that the Supreme Court will never abandon the concept of substantive due process because it is "an ever flowing fount of judicial power."[13]

And so, the power, the clout, the supremacy of the Supreme Court exploded—all because Joseph Lochner did not like labor unions and would not pay his fifty-dollar fine.

CAN THE LONG-TERM IMPLICATIONS OF SUPREME COURT RULINGS BE ANTICIPATED?

Henry Weismann was a hero. The man most responsible for the passage of the Bakeshop Act was hailed as being the one most responsible for eliminating its ten-hour rule. He was praised and rewarded for his achievement. Yet he never again argued a case before either a New York or federal appeals court.

A number of major newspapers editorialized in favor of the decision, but primarily because it was seen as striking a blow against union power and legislative overreach. In contrast, those publications favorable to the growing labor movement were greatly distressed.

The significant legal doctrine given birth by the case was largely overlooked at first. But, it did not take but a few years before reform-minded progressives came to recognize what the Court had done. They began to bemoan the fact that reformers had lost control of the nation's direction. In the decades before *Lochner,* the Progressive Era had unfolded, in fits and spurts, as reformers had hoped. They had succeeded in rallying the public to support laws that addressed the negative side of industrialization and urbanization. With that public support, they enjoyed considerable success in state legislatures. But now, with *Lochner,* they could not be assured that reform legislation would pass judicial muster. They expressed fear that the power had been taken from the people and their elected representatives. In effect, the decision-making process envisioned by the Founders was now in turmoil.

Teddy Roosevelt was the first public figure to draw the public's attention to *Lochner.* Roosevelt was a great reformer. He had energized the nation to make legislative changes—some at the national level, but most at the state level—to address the perceived evils of his age. He claimed that the courts had suddenly become a roadblock to his efforts, and he used his bully pulpit to call out the Justices.

In the decades after *Lochner,* the Supreme Court struck down nearly two hundred laws, mostly state laws, as violations of personal "liberty" as the Court interpreted that term.[14]

It would be wrong, however, to argue that the Supreme Court had taken a side in the reform movement. A review of the decisions, both state and federal, in the decades after *Lochner* shows that a significant number of reform laws were not overturned by the Court. The substantive due process doctrine, as it has been applied by the courts, often resulted in decisions finding many uses of the police power justifiable, even though a liberty interest of one type or another might have been impacted by the legislation.

State prohibitions on perceived immoral conduct such as gambling, drinking, smoking, and prostitution were upheld. Rent control laws following World War I were upheld, along with state laws requiring licenses of certain professions and trades. Laws to encourage commerce and to establish standards of weights and measures were found to be legitimate exercises of the police power, even though they often affected the liberty of contract. Workers Compensation laws, a significant part of the reform era, were upheld, even though the laws dramatically affected the relationship between employees and employers. An Oregon statute limiting the number of hours that women could work was upheld by the Supreme Court just three years after *Lochner.*

It would be wrong to conclude that *Lochner* reflected a political or economic philosophy, as many of its critics have suggested. The mixed results of Court decisions after 1905 belie that argument.

What is unassailable, however, is that the Supreme Court has never altered its belief that it has the ultimate say. The fundamental premise of the substantive due process doctrine, that the Court has veto power over legislation that five or more members of the Court find to be an unreasonable infringement on liberty as they define it, has never been disavowed. That veto power was to be used by Justices of both a liberal and a conservative bent.

In theory, the so-called *Lochner Era,* the several decades after 1905 when substantive due process was relied on to analyze a multitude of cases in the economic arena, ended in 1937 when President Franklin D. Roosevelt's reconfigured Supreme Court abandoned it. Thereafter, the presumption became that any law relying on the police power to protect health, safety, and commerce would pass constitutional muster unless there was absolutely no rational basis for the law. The legislature was given the presumption that it had acted constitutionally. In theory, *Lochner* was dead and buried.

But then, *Lochner* was resurrected in an entirely new arena in the 1960s. A Supreme Court that would be repelled by the use of substantive due process to void a state or federal law in the economic arena found it perfectly acceptable to void a law they disagreed with involving the use of contraceptives. In the 1965 case of *Griswold v. Connecticut,* a majority of the Court discovered a newly existing "right of privacy," a constitutional right that had apparently been hidden from the view of all courts of the United States for nearly two centuries.[15] The case invalidated

Connecticut laws that made it a crime to use, dispense, or counsel the use of contraceptives.

Some in the majority went to great pains to avoid using the language of substantive due process. The majority opinion specifically denied that they looked to *Lochner* for a precedent. But Justices writing concurring opinions openly spoke of the right of privacy existing because of the due process clause of the Fourteenth Amendment. The dissenters in the case called out the Justices in the majority, proclaiming that despite their protestations, those Justices who had discovered the new right to privacy, and then found that the anti-contraception law of Connecticut was an unreasonable infringement of that right, were simply reverting to Lochnerian substantive due process.

Eight years later, in the case of *Roe v. Wade,* the Supreme Court went all out Lochnerian.

A young woman named Norma L. McCorvey wanted to terminate her pregnancy. She lived in the state of Texas, and Texas law prohibited an abortion under the circumstances of her case. She sued, claiming that the Texas abortion statute was unconstitutional. The Supreme Court declared the Texas statute violated the Constitution. By its ruling, the Court upended the abortion statutes in a majority of the states.

The majority refused to acknowledge *Lochner* and substantive due process as the doctrine that it was relying on.[16] However, the majority opinion located the right to privacy in the Fourteenth Amendment's due process "liberty" and noted that it placed limits on state action. The state action in this case, an abortion law, was deemed to have gone beyond the allowable limits of that liberty. This is clearly applying the doctrine of substantive due process. In his concurring opinion, Justice Potter Stewart said so. In his dissent, Justice William Rehnquist said so.

Roe most assuredly did not end the abortion debate. Controversy still agitates the nation today over when and under what circumstances a woman has the right to terminate a pregnancy. States continue to grapple with its nuances four decades later. Courts continue to pass judgment on laws passed to address it. Protests continue to roil our nation.

Subsequently, legal scholars of all stripes acknowledged *Roe* to be nothing if not a modern-day version of *Lochner* in that it relied on the substantive due process doctrine that *Lochner* spawned. Quite remarkably, in some quarters, substantive due process and *Lochner* have been hailed as essential to modern constitutional jurisprudence. One scholar gave a new spin to the case, asserting that *Lochner* was good because it was the source of a strong role for the courts in protecting individual rights; however, *Lochner* was bad in that it protected the rights of individuals in the economic arena, which were the wrong rights to protect.

Subsequent to *Roe,* substantive due process has been employed by the Supreme Court to void state laws in a multitude of areas, including laws that criminalized sodomy. It was the basis upon which the Supreme Court voided the laws of a majority of states that provided protections for traditional marriage, as will be discussed in chapter 7.

During the *Lochner Era,* that period between 1905 and 1937, the critics of the Supreme Court were those who are usually considered liberal or progressive. Those critics savaged the Court for voiding laws that the majority of the Court felt infringed on the individual's right to contract. They criticized the Court for overturning the will of the people as reflected in legislation passed by state legislatures and the Congress of the United States. They accused the Court of being "activist" and "conservative."

Today, the critics of the Supreme Court's decisions such as *Roe* and *Obergefell* are on the other side of the political spectrum. The conservatives are alarmed that laws passed by state legislatures protecting the rights of the unborn and traditional marriage are being voided by the Supreme Court relying on *Lochner*'s substantive due process doctrine.

For over one hundred years, *Lochner* has been a tool used by judges and Justices of all stripes in deciding a multitude of important cases, and each case has triggered condemnation by those who did not like the outcome.

A FINAL THOUGHT

In the *Lochner* opinion, the five Justices in the majority asked the rhetorical question, "Are we all . . . at the mercy of legislative majorities?" The answer to that question would be "yes" if we believe in the system of government created by the Founders. Those who crafted the Constitution believed in a republican form of government, in which the decisions would be made by those elected by the people. The courts were simply to exercise judgment, not to impose the will of the judges. It was believed that the police power of the states would be controlled by the people and those whom they elected to represent them.

The case of Joseph Lochner has clearly altered that formula.

On the day that the case of *Roe v. Wade* was issued in 1973, the Supreme Court handed down a decision in a companion case overturning the abortion law in Georgia. In a stinging dissent in that case, Justice Byron White, appointed to the Supreme Court by President John F. Kennedy, wrote:

> With all due respect, I dissent. I find nothing in the language or history of the Constitution to support the Court's judgments. The Court simply fashions and announces a new constitutional right for pregnant woman and, with scarcely any reason or authority for its action, invests that right with sufficient substance to override most existing state abortion statutes. *The upshot is that the people and the legislatures of the 50 States are constitutionally disentitled to weigh the relative importance of the continued existence and development of the fetus, on the one hand, against a spectrum of possible impacts on the mother, on the other hand.* As an exercise or raw judicial power, the Court perhaps has authority to do what it does today; but in my view its judgment is an improvident and extravagant exercise of the power of judicial review that the Constitution extends to this Court.[17]

Justice White's criticism raises a very important question: Who is best equipped to decide issues fraught with so many considerations and over which reasonable people can disagree?

For good or ill, Joseph Lochner's unwillingness to bend to the efforts of labor unions and to the edict of the courts has answered that question: It is the courts. His decision unquestionably altered the course of the history of this nation and has been the source of the Supreme Court shaping the nation to its will.[18]

NOTES

Epigraph: Bork, *Tempting of America*, 44.

1. For more information about the Progressive Era, see Morison and Commager, *Growth of the American Republic*.
2. Smith, *Wealth of Nations*, 68.
3. *Allgeyer v. Louisiana*, 165 U.S. 578 (1897).
4. *Holden v. Hardy*, 169 U.S. 366 (1898).
5. *Atkin v. Kansas*, 191 U.S. 207 (1903).
6. *Lochner v. New York*, 198 U.S. 45 (1905).
7. See The Library of Congress > Exhibitions > Magna Carta: Muse and Mentor > Due Process of Law.
8. *Lochner*, 53.
9. Ibid., 56–57.
10. George, *Great Cases*, 131.
11. Ibid., 132.
12. *In re Winship*, 397 U.S. 358 (1970), 397.
13. Bork, *Tempting*, 32.
14. *Obergefell v. Hodges*, 135 S.Ct. 2584, 2617 (2015).
15. *Griswold v. Connecticut*, 381 U.S. 479 (1965).
16. *Roe v. Wade*, 410 U.S. 113 (1973).
17. *Doe v. Bolton*, 410 U.S. 179, 221–222 (1973); emphasis added.
18. For information on the case of *Lochner v. New York*, see Bernstein, *Centennial Retrospective*; Bernstein, *Rehabilitating Lochner*; Bork, *Tempting*; Kens, *Lochner*; George, *Great Cases*.

CHAPTER FOUR

HOW 12 ACRES OF WHEAT LED TO AN ALL-POWERFUL WASHINGTON, D.C.

WICKARD V. FILBURN (1942)

"Were we directed from Washington when to sow,
and when to reap, we should soon want bread."

—*Thomas Jefferson*

"A MORE PERFECT UNION"

The first enumerated purpose of the Constitution of the United States, as stated in its Preamble, is to "form a more perfect Union." More perfect than what? More perfect than that union of the states under the Articles of Confederation, the governmental framework under which the United States had operated in its first decade. The Articles of Confederation had created a system in which the national government was too weak and the states too independent. It was failing.

Was a "perfect union" the goal, a union where the states were assimilated and rendered insignificant and irrelevant under an all-powerful national government? No, the Founders did not want all power to reside in the national government. Under this "more perfect, yet not total union," the states were to retain a substantial amount of sovereignty and a significant degree of primacy.

This system of shared power was not the result of a grand compromise or a begrudging surrender to the states. It was a conscious decision made for a specific purpose.

The Founders of this nation designed a system of government with the specific goal of avoiding tyranny as they defined it—the destruction of liberty by a government taking rights that the people had not voluntarily surrendered to it. They perceived that the threat of tyranny emanated from both the state and the national governments.

The Founders feared that the states might be overtaken by undemocratic factions, be they majority groups or minority groups. Such factions could extinguish the liberty of the people at the state level just as they could at the national level. To reduce such a possibility, the Constitution required that the United States guarantee to every state a republican form of government and protection against domestic violence.[1]

The Founders were much more concerned, however, with the possibility of a national government becoming too powerful. They had just removed themselves from the tyranny of a government located several thousand miles away across the Atlantic Ocean. They were not about to lose their hard-fought-for liberty by surrendering it to a national government a few hundred or a thousand miles away, wherever the new government was to find itself seated.

To eliminate that threat, a national government with three distinct branches, each capable of checking and balancing the power of the other, was conceived.

The Founders also believed that by limiting the powers possessed by the national government to a few and retaining the bulk of the governing power in the states, the national government could never become a threat to personal liberty. They consciously limited the power of the national government to those specific powers enumerated or itemized in the Constitution.

As James Madison argued in support of ratification of the Constitution in *The Federalist,* those powers that were delegated to the national government "were few and defined. Those which are to remain in the State governments are numerous and indefinite."[2] The enumerated powers of the national government were those that were necessary to protect the nation and to conduct foreign affairs, "war, peace, negotiation, and foreign commerce."[3] Those powers that were reserved to the states were those of immediate importance to the people in conducting their ordinary lives, those matters involving daily living, liberty, property, public order, and prosperity.

Important in the Founders' notion of protection from tyranny, their plan called for the national government to be checked by the states, and the states were to be checked by the national government. It was their firm belief that by dividing power between the states and the national government, the threat to liberty would be reduced, if not eliminated.

This balancing and checking of the state and national governments was called Federalism. In its aim to preserve the liberty of the people, it was a new and unique system, untried and untested in the history of the world.

The genius of Federalism was expressed well by Alexander Hamilton. In the debate at the ratifying convention of the state of New York, in his effort to convince delegates not to fear the power of the national government under the Constitution, he reasoned:

> The State governments possess inherent advantages, which will ever give them an influence and ascendancy over the National Government, and will for ever preclude the possibility of federal encroachments. That their liberties, indeed, can be subverted by the federal head, is repugnant to every rule of political calculation.[4]

Later, he continued with his argument:

> The balance between the National and State governments ought to be dwelt on with peculiar attention, as it is of the utmost importance. It forms a double security to the people. If one encroaches on their rights they will find a powerful protection in the other. Indeed, they will both be prevented from overpassing their constitutional limits by a certain rivalship, which will ever subsist between them.[5]

Has that rivalship endured? Have the states remained ascendant over the national government? Are they even viable players in the scheme of Federalism today? Of critical importance, have the states retained the power and the ability to stop the national government from encroaching on the liberty of the people?

Looking at the relative positions of the national government and the states today, it is quite clear that one dominates the other. Power and influence have flowed toward Washington, D.C., and away from the states at a steady rate since the 1930s. This has occurred as Congress and the President have made laws that inflated the powers and influence of the national government. With very few exceptions, such laws have been endorsed and upheld by the Supreme Court of the United States.

Federalism is now a shadow of what was intended by the Founders.

Arguably, this centralization of power and influence in our nation's capital is a necessary evolution, one essential to meet the demands of our interconnected and interdependent modern world. That is a subjective matter not for this book to contest nor to support.

What this book *does* attempt is to explain how this reshaping of America came to be—specifically, the role that the Supreme Court of the United States played in that restructuring.

Although it is just one among many cases that endorsed presidential and congressional destruction of Federalism, *Wickard v. Filburn* is acknowledged to be the case that moved the boundary of federal domination over the states to its most outward limits. More significant, especially from the perspective of the Founders, *Wickard* sanctioned a dramatic expansion of the authority of the national government to tell average Americans how to live their lives. The means by which this came about was through the Commerce Power in the Constitution of the United States.

THE COMMERCE POWER

One of the enumerated powers given to the Congress by the Constitution is the power to "regulate Commerce with foreign Nations, and among the several States, and with Indian Tribes."[6] Although it is not the only enumerated power that the national government has used to expand its influence, it is the one that has been relied upon most frequently and most effectively.

Congress has relied on the Commerce Power to justify the regulation of nearly all commercial activity—not just activities between and among the states, but those that are conducted exclusively within a state. It was relied upon in 1970 to freeze all wages and prices in the United States. It has been used to justify a variety of federal laws not directly connected to commerce: for example, the civil rights legislation of the last half century and all environmental protection legislation.

The Commerce Power has been the means by which Congress has dramatically altered the realm of criminal law. Historically, almost all crimes were prosecuted by the states. In recent decades, relying on the Commerce Power, Congress has turned an untold number of activities and actions into violations of federal criminal laws and regulations. This assumption of power by the federal government to prosecute citizens criminally is a dramatic reshaping of the American criminal justice system.

In sum, the Commerce Power has been the primary means by which power has shifted away from the states and to Washington, D.C.

How did it come to be?

In the first hundred years of our nation's existence, the national government made little effort to interpose itself into the regulation of business and commerce. It respected the concept of Federalism and did not interfere with the power vested in the states to regulate those commercial activities that took place within a state, such as mining, agriculture, and manufacturing.

After the American Civil War, as the Industrial Revolution unfolded, Congress saw the need to regulate some commerce in order to meet the challenges of industrialization. The first major piece of legislation it passed was the Interstate Commerce Act of 1887. It was approved to deal with the rising power and influence of railroads.

As railroads emerged as the primary mode of transporting both people and commercial goods, abuses were inevitable. Agreements among railroads that eliminated competition, thus permitting railroad companies to charge whatever prices they wanted, became common. The Interstate Commerce Act authorized the creation of the Interstate Commerce Commission. This commission was given the power to regulate railroad shipping rates; but, in deference to Federalism, its power extended only to setting the rates charged on railroad lines that operated between states.

The Sherman Antitrust Act followed in 1890. Its intent was to prohibit monopolies in business and industry by way of "trusts." In the first case the Supreme Court heard concerning this act, the Court paid due deference to Federalism. It drew a sharp distinction between those activities that the Court perceived to be for the states to regulate, such as manufacturing, agriculture, mining, and similar businesses, and those for the national government to regulate, which included the movement between states of the products or yields of those businesses.[7]

In 1918, the Supreme Court further limited the power of Congress to regulate under the Commerce Power. In this instance, Congress had relied on the Commerce Power to bring about a major social reform by banning the interstate flow of goods manufactured by child labor. The Court ruled that the regulation of child labor was for the states and not the federal government. In doing so, it recognized Federalism and the necessity of limiting the power of Congress in matters that fell primarily within state regulatory authority.[8]

Although the Supreme Court was not always consistent in its rulings, as the nation approached its sesquicentennial, the Court had managed to reserve to the states a significant role in regulating manufacturing, mining, agriculture, and business. The role of the federal government remained limited to regulating the movement of goods and products interstate or between states.

THE SUPREME COURT IS "REFORMED"

But the nation then encountered the Great Depression. The election of Franklin D. Roosevelt led to consideration of vigorous legislation at the national level to deal with the fearful days the nation then faced. These bills often attempted to regulate some areas of business and commerce that previous Courts had deemed to be within the exclusive regulatory authority of the states. In the early years of Roosevelt's "New Deal," the Supreme Court struck down much of this legislation as being beyond the Commerce Power of Congress. Often the decisions were 5–4 splits. In those early years of the 1930s, the Supreme Court was regarded as a major obstacle to President Roosevelt's efforts to lift the nation out of its serious economic crisis.

After he was reelected to his second term in 1936, Roosevelt moved aggressively to remove that obstacle. He proposed legislation to increase the size of the Supreme Court to as many as fifteen Justices so that he could "pack" the Court with new and sympathetic members. The legislation was introduced in February of 1937. The proposal was not well received by those in Congress, even though the President had just been reelected by a crushing margin and the Congress was overwhelmingly of the same party. Despite the fact that its prospects for actually becoming law were dim, the message the President intended to send in proposing the "Court-packing" legislation was received by at least one member of the Court.

Within months a truly amazing and quite unexpected series of rulings emanated from the Supreme Court. On March 29, 1937, the Court handed down a decision approving a minimum wage law in Washington state. The margin was 5–4. One Justice had switched, for this decision reversed a ruling that the Court had made just nine months earlier when it invalidated New York's similar wage law. Two weeks later, again by a 5–4 vote, the Court issued five decisions upholding the National Labor Relations Act. Six weeks later, the Court found the Social Security Act constitutional with the same five-member majority.

The "Court packing" legislation did not pass, but the Court had been changed without it. Within five years, through retirements and deaths, Roosevelt had named seven new members to the Court, and his desired transformation was complete.

The power of Congress was expanding exponentially. The Supreme Court was endorsing laws that granted Congress power over all areas of commerce, including the ability to bring about labor and social reforms under the pretext of regulating commerce. It appeared that there were no limits to the authority of Congress to legislate relying on the Commerce Power.

Were there any limits? Roscoe C. Filburn was going to find out.

THE DEPRESSION AND THE FARMERS

It is fitting that a fight over farm policy led to the Supreme Court's decision that expanded the power of the federal government. The ebbs and flows of agriculture had been the primary cause of our nation's economic expansion and contraction since the beginning of the United States. Farming had largely determined the nation's economic well-being. Agriculture's travails were a major cause of the Great Depression.

Ironically, the period just one generation before the Great Depression could be deemed "Golden Years" for farmers. In the first decades of the twentieth century, prices on products were high, interest rates on borrowed money were low, and times were good.

Nearly 40 percent of the total national workforce was still engaged in agriculture. The population of the United States remained mostly rural; in fact, it was not until 1920 that there were more people living in cities than in rural areas.

But World War I triggered changes in agriculture that were dramatic. The beginning of the war in Europe collapsed prices for wheat and cotton as Europe cut back on imports. When the United States entered the war three years later, there was an immediate push to increase farm production domestically. Forty million acres of new farmland were opened up in the Midwest, more wheat came to market, and wheat prices collapsed even more with the creation of a massive surplus.

In the years after the war, more long-term and quite fundamental changes were in store. Mechanization came to the farm. This made it easier to grow crops and to farm more land. At the same time, the elimination of real horsepower reduced the amount of grain being consumed. Again, wheat farmers suffered the most.

Exports were vital to America's farmers. In the years after World War I, the export markets were mauled. Political upheaval played a major role in the collapse of some exports, particularly in Germany, Italy, and Russia. Some nations responded to the cries of their own suffering farmers by imposing tariffs on agricultural products imported into their nations. Foolishly, the United States followed suit. In 1930, the United

States Congress passed the Smoot-Hawley Tariff Act, imposing import tariffs on a large number of agricultural products. This action by the United States was then responded to in kind by even more members of the international community.

Supplies continued to soar in the United States, and prices fell even further. Farmers were being driven into poverty in mass numbers. Foreclosures became rampant. On one day in 1932, one-quarter of the farmland in the state of Mississippi was transferred by foreclosure auctions. Farmers rose up in civil disobedience to the foreclosure disaster.

In 1930, nearly one in five workers in America was working in agriculture. Almost 8 percent of the total gross domestic product of the United States was derived from agriculture. The collapse of the agriculture segment of the total economy sent many millions into the lines of the unemployed. This collapse was a direct cause of the Great Depression.

When Franklin D. Roosevelt first ran for President in 1932, he promised as one of his key campaign planks to save the farms and farmers. After his election, he was able to get the Congress to act, but most legislation it passed was rejected by the Supreme Court.

But then the Court was transformed.

Thereafter, Congress was reenergized. It set about to pass legislation that had been rejected by the Supreme Court as beyond its power. It passed for a second time four pieces of legislation to deal with the crises in agriculture; the first three were all challenged in court and were upheld. The last to be contested was the Agriculture Adjustment Act of 1938. This was when Roscoe C. Filburn entered the picture.

ROSCOE C. FILBURN—OHIO FARMER OF CONSIDERABLE REPUTE

Roscoe C. Filburn was a farmer in Ohio. In this he was following in the footsteps of four previous generations of Filburns. As with many farmers, Roscoe C. Filburn took tremendous pride in his independence. He was known to brag that he had never worked for another man in his entire life.

Was he a big farmer? No, in fact he milked a few cows, sold some milk, and drank the rest. He raised a few chickens and sold eggs. He might have enjoyed seventy-five customers a day.

So what brought him to the attention of federal authorities in 1941? Every fall, Farmer Filburn would plant some wheat. When that wheat was harvested the next year, he would eat some of it, he would feed some of it to his animals, he would save some for planting the next year, and if he had some left over he would sell it in the local market. Because all of his wheat was used on his farm or sold locally, he did not see himself engaged in interstate commerce.

In 1940, Filburn was told by federal officials that he was allowed to plant only 11.1 acres of wheat for the 1941 harvest. That decree was issued pursuant to the Agricultural Adjustment Act of 1938, an act intended to bring an end to surpluses in agricultural crops, which depressed the price that farmers received for those crops. It empowered the Secretary of Agriculture to decide each year how many acres of wheat could be planted for the next year in all of the United States. The target was to grow just enough wheat that the price the farmers would be paid would be reasonable. Each and every farmer was then given an allotment of that national total.

But Filburn did not like being told what to do by the government in Washington, D.C. As a farmer, he was instinctively independent. He violated the edict and planted more wheat than he was permitted—in fact, he planted all of twenty-three acres. When he harvested his wheat the next year, he brought in 239 more bushels of wheat than the Secretary of Agriculture had authorized. For that offense, he was fined $117.11. He filed suit in a federal district court challenging his penalty. He named as the defendant Mr. Claude R. Wickard, the U.S. Secretary of Agriculture.

THE SUPREME COURT DECIDES ROSCOE FILBURN'S FATE

The case ultimately ended up before the Supreme Court of the United States. In the brief filed for Filburn before that Court, his lawyers issued a very stark warning: If the Court accepted the arguments of the Secretary of Agriculture, the limits intended by the Founders on the power and authority of the Congress of the United States would be nullified.

Despite that dire warning, the Supreme Court was to find for the Secretary of Agriculture.

The Court ruled that in exercising its Commerce Power, Congress was not limited to the regulation of products and produce moving between states. All the former tests relied upon by the Supreme Court to limit the Congress under the Commerce Power were to be discarded. No longer was there to be given deference to those areas that had been reserved in the original Constitution for the states to regulate.

The Court said that Congress had the authority under the Constitution to regulate any and all economic activities, even though completely local, and in fact not even commerce, if that activity wielded a "substantial economic effect on interstate commerce." It did not matter if that effect was indirect or circumstantial.

How, one might ask, would Roscoe C. Filburn's growing a couple of extra acres of wheat wield a "substantial economic effect on interstate commerce"?

The Court said that even homegrown and home-consumed wheat had an economic effect because that wheat figured into the total amount of wheat that was available for markets. In consuming his own wheat, or choosing not to consume it, Filburn was deducting from or adding to the total amount of wheat on the open market.

How might Filburn's inconsequential 239 bushels of wheat affect that amount available for the massive national or even more massive international market?

The Court answered that the regulation of even a couple of hundred bushels of wheat, as Roscoe C. Filburn was responsible for raising, was justified because if you took his small amount of surplus wheat and multiplied it by the hundreds and thousands and tens of thousands of similar small farmers combined, you would have a major impact on the amount of wheat available in the larger national or international market.

In sum, in order for Congress to accomplish its goal of stabilizing the price of wheat, it was a legitimate exercise of its Commerce Power to regulate all wheat, no matter where it was going to be consumed, even if it was never going to be shipped interstate and was never going to be part of commerce but instead was just going to be eaten by Roscoe C. Filburn and his family, his cows, and his chickens.

The Supreme Court set two parameters for defining the reach of the Commerce Power: first, any economic activity, no matter how local, no matter how far removed from actual interstate commerce it may be, if that economic activity has a substantial impact on interstate commerce, it is within the power of Congress to regulate; and second, substantial impact must be calculated by adding together everyone who engages in such activity and everything they might produce.

With such parameters in play, there are very few human activities that fall outside the power of Congress to regulate under the Commerce Power.

For example, let us take household baked cookies. When a member of a family bakes cookies, he or she is replacing those that might be purchased at a store. A lot of people bake cookies. The cumulative effect of people baking their own cookies is great on the total market of manufactured cookies. Therefore, under the reasoning of *Wickard,* Congress could regulate the household baking of cookies. Congress may not have chosen to regulate the number of cookies each household can bake each week, but under the formula relied upon in *Wickard,* it could.

Wickard v. Filburn was the finale in the Supreme Court's reversal of its view of the Commerce Power. This reversal had taken place in less than one decade. The reversal was so far-reaching, so complete, that it could be argued that it constituted an amendment to the Constitution without the inconvenience of following the amendment process.

By this and related rulings, the Supreme Court has abandoned the historical distinctions under Federalism. It has given carte blanche authority for Congress to regulate all production as well as transportation. The states have been squeezed out of their historical role of regulating mining, agriculture, manufacturing, and such.

Again, even though Congress is not regulating the baking of cookies, since *Wickard* it has taken to the regulation of an incalculable amount of human activity.[9]

> HOW MUCH POWER IS THE SUPREME COURT
> WILLING TO HAVE AMASSED BY
> THE FEDERAL GOVERNMENT?

ROSCOE C. FILBURN'S LEGACY

It is ironic that Roscoe C. Filburn's effort to restrict the power of Congress to regulate the daily affairs of Americans resulted in a decision that stretched that power beyond comprehension.

Following *Filburn,* it was going to be nearly six decades before the Supreme Court rendered a decision saying that Congress had gone too far expanding its reach under the Commerce Power.

In the interim, no holds were barred. The federal government now regulates every aspect of commercial activity in the United States. If state regulation is inconsistent with a federal law or regulation, the state regulation is voided.

Besides the unfettered regulation of economic activity by the federal government, and the assertion of primacy over state regulation, the Supreme Court has sanctioned Congressional expansion of noncommercial activities under the guise of the exercise of the Commerce Power.

For example, the Court reversed its 1918 decision and ultimately decided that Congress can prohibit the interstate shipment of goods produced by employees making too little in wages, or working more than forty hours a week, or using child labor. In 1918, the Supreme Court had said that in such matters as wages and labor conditions, the states had supremacy. The reformed Supreme Court saw it differently.

As described in chapter 2 of this book, there had been a lengthy discussion regarding the Civil Rights Act of 1875. That crucial legislation had been held to be unconstitutional because the Court found that it was not justified under the Fourteenth Amendment. No consideration of it being justified by the Commerce Power was argued for. Ninety years later, Congress passed the Civil Rights Act of 1964. It was immediately challenged for its constitutionality. The question considered by the Court was whether the refusal of a motel or restaurant to serve an African-American was a burden on interstate commerce and thus subject to regulation by Congress. The Court concluded that it was, and therefore was within the power of Congress under the Commerce Clause.

During the period of unfettered expansion of federal power, there were some on the Supreme Court who objected. The concept of Federalism, although on its deathbed, still had some Justices who believed in its necessity. In a 1985 case in which the Court decided that federal minimum wage and overtime provisions could be forced on the state governments, four Justices dissented and noted that: "A unique feature of the United States is the *federal* system of government guaranteed by the Constitution and implicit in the very name of our country. Despite some genuflecting in the Court's opinion to the concept of federalism, today's decision effectively reduces the Tenth Amendment to meaningless rhetoric when Congress acts pursuant to the Commerce Clause."[10]

They were voices in the wilderness.

THE CONGRESS, CRIME, AND THE COMMERCE POWER

Historically, one of the areas reserved to the states under their general police power is the power to define what acts constitute a crime and what punishment should be meted out for that crime. In 1971, in the case of *Perez v. United States,* the Supreme Court held that under the Commerce Clause, Congress has the nearly unlimited authority to define federal crimes.[11]

That decision is important for reasons in addition to its obvious impact on Federalism.

The Founders fully understood that the power of the government to prosecute someone criminally is a potent and dangerous weapon. They themselves had been victimized by that power in the hands of the King of England. In the Declaration of Independence, the Founders listed those offenses that the Crown had inflicted on the citizens of the American colonies. Among those that Thomas Jefferson presented as evidence of the King's intention to establish an absolute tyranny over the American people was, "He has made Judges dependent on his Will alone . . . For depriving us in many cases, of the benefits of Trial by Jury: For transporting us beyond Seas to be tried for pretended offences."[12]

Criminal prosecutions are a most effective way of attacking, even destroying people whom the government does not like or whom it might fear. That was how the King of England had used that power. It is also a most effective way of stifling unpopular movements—as the King had attempted. Individuals and groups who can be criminally prosecuted for purely political reasons are vulnerable to the extreme.

In addition to the very healthy fear of abuse by the government, the Founders had a strong belief in the importance of protecting innocence in criminal matters. An example to illustrate this belief is that of John Adams and his willingness to represent the British soldiers who were defendants in the infamous "Boston Massacre."

In March of 1770, anger and frustration aimed at the British military presence in Boston were at a high point. That winter night, a mob surrounded a group of British soldiers outside the British Custom House. When the mob began to pelt the soldiers with snow, then ice and stones, the soldiers opened fire. Five members of the mob were killed.

The soldiers were brought to trial for murder. No one was willing to represent them except for a young lawyer named John Adams. He was warned by many not to take the case. He was notified that his budding law practice would be in jeopardy, and most certainly any political future would be darkened by his willingness to defend the hated soldiers. But Adams firmly believed that every person in a free country was entitled to a sound defense in a criminal trial.

In the two trials that followed, John Adams obtained not-guilty verdicts for the officer in charge of the soldiers and acquittal of six of the eight soldiers. The two who were found guilty were convicted of manslaughter, and the punishment was the branding of their thumbs.

Adams's argument for his clients, and the justification for his taking the case, included the very profound belief that it was far better that many guilty persons go free than that one innocent person be unjustly punished. "The reason is, because it's of more importance to community, that innocence should be protected, than it is, that guilt should be punished."[13]

John Adams was not the only one who held this opinion. It is not happenstance that in the first ten amendments to the Constitution of the United States, that which we call the Bill of Rights, thirteen of the twenty-three separate rights listed pertain to the rights of criminal defendants. The Founders were relentless in their effort to stop the government from using the power of criminal prosecutions arbitrarily and unjustly.

The evidence is also overwhelming that the Founders did not intend that the power and authority of criminal prosecutions be held by the national government. In the Constitution itself, the Congress was granted authority to make criminal only the acts of treason, offenses committed on federal property, counterfeiting, offenses against the Law of Nations, piracy, and felonies committed on the high seas. This is wholly consistent with the Founders' understanding that matters dealing with the internal order of the states were for the states themselves. This was at the very core of what Federalism meant to them.

But over time, that changed. As the national government grew in its power, it expanded its reach into the area of criminal law and prosecutions. Originally, such expansions were to criminalize offenses of an interstate nature, that is, where criminals took their victims across state lines. For example, in the early 1900s, Congress passed the Mann Act, which made it a federal crime to transport a woman across state lines for purposes of prostitution.

In the era of Prohibition, the 1920s, federal criminal laws were passed to enforce the Eighteenth Amendment. During this era, federal criminal prosecutions exploded. That came to an end when the Twenty-First Amendment was passed in 1933 and Prohibition was abolished.

In the decades that followed, more crimes were federalized, but there was always an interstate component to the crime; for example, it was made a federal crime to transport stolen property across state lines.

But after the *Perez* case of 1971, Congress stepped up its federalization of crimes under the auspices of the Commerce Power. Such action has been endorsed by the Supreme Court.

Congress has not always created new crimes. Often it has simply made federal crimes of those acts that had historically been state crimes; it has essentially duplicated state criminal law.

But beyond the duplication of historical state criminal law, the passing of laws to regulate so many aspects of the lives and activities of the American citizen and business has resulted in an explosion of regulations, many of which are enforced with criminal sanctions.

Today, no one knows how many federal laws and regulations there are that contain criminal penalties. They are scattered throughout fifty different Titles of the United States Code and 175,000 pages of the Code of Federal Regulations.[14] There are quite simply too many to count.

Some have tried. Their conclusions are never precise. One study concluded that in 2004 there were more than 4,000 offenses with criminal penalties in the United States Code. By 2007, the number had grown to 4,450. If all federal regulations are considered, one estimate says that there are 10,000 potential federal criminal laws and regulations. Another study says over 300,000 federal regulations could be enforced criminally.

The vast majority of these crimes, both statutory and regulatory, have come about since 1970, and all are based on the broad Commerce Power of the Congress.

The potential for the types of abuses feared by the Founders is very, very real.

How is an average citizen of this country expected to know how and when his or her conduct is criminal under any of 4,000, 10,000, or 300,000 possible criminal acts?

One author has speculated that the average citizen in this nation could be guilty of violating multiple federal felony statutes in an average day without even knowing it.[15]

Throughout history, it has been understood that for one to be found guilty of a crime, there had to be an intent to commit the crime, what is known in the law as *mens rea*. That requirement under the common law was reaffirmed as a requirement of modern, statutory criminal statues in a 1952 decision by the United States Supreme Court. In that opinion, the Court stated that before one could be convicted of a crime there had to be proven "an evil-meaning mind with an evil-doing hand."[16]

Despite this, in an evaluation of the 446 nonviolent, non-drug-related criminal laws introduced in the 109th Congress (2005–2007) and which members of Congress considered for passage, more than half lacked a requirement that the person committing the crime acted with a criminal intent.[17]

Some of those who have attempted to quantify the numbers have been frustrated to the point of exhaustion because of the complexity of the federal laws and regulations. Even those who are schooled in the law, and who undertake to carefully examine and master the laws and regulations, cannot do so. What of the average citizen? It has long been a principle of the criminal law that fair warning must be given to ordinary persons, in language understandable by them, of the potential of a criminal violation if they pass a certain line. That fair warning often does not exist in the world of federal criminal law and regulations today.

One of the greatest dangers from the federalization of crimes is the very real situation in which a defendant is tried in both state court and federal court for the same criminal conduct. This is permitted, despite the double jeopardy clause of the Constitution (which prohibits a person from being prosecuted twice for the same crime) because the state and national governments are deemed to be separate sovereigns. An example of such is a case in which a person is convicted in state court of assaulting a victim and prosecuted separately in federal court for having used a camera that traveled in interstate commerce to record the assault. Separate crimes, separate trials, and separate and consecutive prison sentences were imposed.

There are critics of this federalization of crime. In his 1998 Year-End Report on the Federal Judiciary, then–Chief Justice William Rehnquist condemned the efforts by Congress to federalize crimes that had traditionally been handled in state courts. He expressed the fear that the trend would change entirely the nature of our federal system. He also decried the obvious political motivation of the Congress, accusing them of appearing responsive to every highly publicized crime by passing legislation making it a federal crime.[18]

His criticism was ignored.

As far back as 1940, fair-minded federal prosecutors were aware of the power that was being accumulated in their hands. This was long before the explosion of federal criminal statutes and regulations. In that year, the new Attorney General of the United States, Robert Jackson, warned his underlings at the Department of Justice of the power they possessed to pick and choose their cases and thus their defendants. He warned against selecting someone to prosecute and then searching the statutes and regulations for a crime to prosecute them for.

As real as that possibility was in 1940, it is much more real today.

It is important to understand that it is not just evil-minded prosecutors who might abuse their power to prosecute. To the contrary, as esteemed lawyer and jurist Louis Brandeis pointed out:

> Experience should teach us to be most on our guard to protect liberty when the Government's purposes are beneficent. Men born to freedom are naturally alert to repel invasion of their liberty by evil-minded rulers. The greatest dangers to liberty lurk in insidious encroachment by men of zeal, well-meaning but without understanding.[19]

A nation founded on the principle that it was the states that should deal with internal order—crime and criminals—has seen a dramatic move away from that principle. That same nation whose Founders took the utmost care to protect the innocent from unjust criminal prosecution and penalties has been reshaped in the last half century because of the green light given to Congress by a compliant judiciary.[20]

THE COMMERCE POWER MEETS ITS LIMITS

From 1937 until 1995, the Supreme Court endorsed every expansion of the power of the federal government by way of the Commerce Power. In 1995, however, the Court found an instance in which Congress had gone too far. The Congressional action in question made it a federal crime to possess a gun within a zone around schools. The 5–4 opinion simply stated that possessing a gun in a gun-free zone had nothing to do with commerce. The dissenters in the case cited *Wickard* to argue that Congress was well within its authority.[21]

Five years later, in a case involving a federal law that gave victims of gender-motivated violence the right to sue in federal court, a five-member majority again found that Congress had exceeded its authority under the Commerce Clause. The Court found no commercial activity in the cases of gender-motivated violence, as sad as such violence might be. *Wickard* figured prominently in the discussion of both the majority and the dissenters.[22]

The most important recent case defining the power of Congress under the Commerce Clause was the Court's review of the constitutionality of the individual mandate provision of the Patient Protection and Affordable Care Act of 2010. This legislation is often referred to as Obamacare.

One of the requirements of that law was that everyone in the United States must purchase a health insurance policy with a minimum level of coverage. Congress relied on the Commerce Power to impose that obligation. It was the finding of the Congress that the failure of so many people to carry health insurance did have a substantial effect on commerce because the costs of providing for the medical care of the uninsured was being shifted to others. In that respect, this case was very different from the 1995 and 2000 decisions, in which the laws in question had no connection to commerce.

Leading up to the Supreme Court's judgment, it was assumed by most legal scholars that Congress was well within its authority. When a lower court judge found that Congress had exceeded its power, the judge was mocked by one law professor who asserted that the judge understood the Constitution less well than his law students.[23]

The question that the Court had to decide was whether Congress had the power not just to regulate the economic activities of the people, such as growing wheat, but to make citizens do something that they had chosen not to do. In this case, that something was to buy a health insurance policy. The bare, five-member majority found that forcing citizens to engage in an activity, in contrast to regulating them once they became engaged, was going too far.

In the majority opinion, an effort was made to demonstrate how far-reaching, even outrageous, were the possibilities if Congress had no limit to its power to tell citizens of this nation what they must do. The Justices used the example of unhealthy eating habits, including obesity, which the Court said was a bigger problem in America than Americans without health insurance. What if Congress decided, they speculated, to solve the problem of unhealthy eating and obesity by passing a law forcing everyone to eat vegetables?

They noted that if Congress could simply mandate a purchase to solve any problem, it would fundamentally transform the relationship between the government and the people. "That is not the country the Framers of our Constitution envisioned."[24]

So, for now, Congress may be able to regulate the baking of cookies, but they cannot make you bake them.

To reach its conclusion, the majority had to distinguish *Wickard,* whereas the dissenters relied on it, showing the fact that Roscoe C. Filburn's decision to grow those extra acres of wheat remains one of the most significant and enduring decisions in our nation's history.

WHERE ARE WE?

The Founders of this nation envisioned a system of government in which tyranny would be contained by certain checks and balances. Chief among them was Federalism, the distribution of power between the states and the national government, with the ability of each to check the other should one seek to take the rights of the citizens not voluntarily granted.

They also envisioned a system in which the national government had very little authority over the people and almost no impact on the daily lives of the people. To the extent government was to interfere with how people went about their everyday lives, that interference would come from local and state governments, governments well within the reach and influence of the people.

That system of government no longer exists.

In deciding *Wickard v. Filburn* as it did, the Supreme Court sanctioned and endorsed a flow of power and influence to Washington, D.C., never contemplated by the framers of the Constitution. One wonders if this would leave the Founders shocked and dismayed at how their grand vision failed.

NOTES

Epigraph: *Autobiography*, in Spalding, ed., *Founders' Almanac*, 153.
1. Article IV, Section 4.
2. Hamilton, Jay, and Madison, *Federalist*, 252.
3. Ibid.
4. Alexander Hamilton, speech delivered at the New York Ratifying Convention, June 20, 1788; quoted in Spalding, *Founders' Almanac*, 154.
5. Ibid.
6. Article I, Section 8.
7. *United States v. E.C. Knight Company*, 156 U.S. 1 (1895).
8. *Hammer v. Dagenhart*, 247 U.S. 251 (1918).
9. For more information on the history of the Commerce Clause and agriculture in the United States, the transformation of the Supreme Court, and the actors and the case itself, see Chen, "Filburn's Legacy"; Chen, "Story"; Dimitri, Effland,

and Conklin, "20th Century Transformation"; Rossum and Tarr, *American Constitutional Law; Wickard v. Filburn,* 63 S.Ct. 82 (1942).

10. *Garcia v. San Antonia Metropolitan Transit Authority,* 469 U.S. 528, 559–560 (1985).

11. *Perez v. United States,* 402 U.S. 146 (1971).

12. Jefferson, "Declaration of Independence."

13. McCullough, *John Adams,* 68.

14. The Code of Federal Regulations is the codification of all federal rules and regulations. It is a multivolume publication containing more than 175,000 pages.

15. Silvergate, *Three Felonies,* xxxvi.

16. *Morissette v. United States,* 342 U.S. 246, 251 (1952); quoted in Silvergate, *Three Felonies,* xxxv.

17. Ibid., xxii.

18. Suro, "Rehnquist Decries Shift."

19. *Olmstead v. United States,* 277 U.S. 438, 479 (1928).

20. For more information on the federalization of criminal law, see Ashdown, "Federalism"; Baker and Bennett, "Measuring Explosive Growth"; Beale, "Federalizing Crime"; Erlich, "Increasing Federalization"; Silvergate, *Three Felonies.*

21. *United States v. Lopez,* 514 U.S. 549 (1995).

22. *United States v. Morrison,* 529 U.S. 598 (2000).

23. Amar, "Constitutional Showdown."

24. *National Federation of Independent Business et al. v. Sebelius,* 132 S.Ct. 2566, 2589 (2012).

CHAPTER FIVE

HOW A NATION FOUNDED BY DEVOUT MEN AND WOMEN CAME TO BAN RELIGION FROM THE PUBLIC ARENA

EVERSON V. BOARD OF EDUCATION OF EWING TOWNSHIP (1947)

"Statesmen, my dear Sir, may plan and speculate for Liberty, but it is Religion and Morality alone, which can establish the Principles upon which Freedom can securely stand."

—*John Adams*

THE FOUNDERS, MORALITY, AND SELF-GOVERNMENT

Those who founded this nation enjoyed a twin blessing: a rare combination of opportunity and insight.

Their opportunity was that they were in a position to create a government of their own making, something entirely new, a government to fit the people and the times they were in. They were not inheriting a government that they could only tinker with. They were not taking a government of someone else's design and amending it. They could and did start from scratch. Their vehicle was the Constitution of the United States. They crafted that document to implement the insight they collectively possessed.

That insight was an uncanny understanding of human nature. For example, they understood that in order for a people to govern themselves, there had to be constraints on the natural predisposition toward tyranny. They understood that in a pure democracy the majority could and would deprive the minority of their rights. They understood that it was possible for a highly motivated minority to gain power over the majority. They understood that power corrupts and that those in power must be constrained by checks and balances and sovereignty shared by the state and federal governments.

The most important of their insights was their understanding that for self-government to succeed, with the maximum amount of liberty and freedom available for enjoyment by the people, the people had to be of a certain character. They had to be a virtuous and moral people.

The reason why is evident to any parent of a teenager. A teenager who is responsible, stays away from trouble, sets his or her own reasonable schedule, is motivated to do homework without being nagged, and so on, likely does not have many rules imposed upon him or her. Such a teen is far freer than a peer whose rebellious nature triggers strict regulation and hovering oversight from a concerned parent.

The same is true of a citizenry. People to whom the rule of law is acceptable and who by nature are disciplined and obedient to universal principles of morality do not need an excessive number of laws and regulations to govern them. Moral people will conduct themselves in such a way, even when the law does not demand it, that the society does not suffer. Moral people will conduct themselves in such a way, when that conduct is neither easily discernible nor discoverable, that society does not suffer.

In sum, a moral people can live their lives free of laws, regulations, and the heavy hand of government because they truly govern themselves.

The Founders understood this.

What is meant by morality? Morality can be understood as that set of moral principles to which a majority of the citizenry subscribes. It is a consensus of what constitutes good behavior. Those who obey those principles are deemed to be moral, and those who do not are deemed to be immoral.

One can create a list of such moral principles that have been part of the moral code of the American people; it is likely such a list would include the traits of truthfulness, honesty, duty, personal responsibility, unselfishness, loyalty, honor, compassion, and courage.[1]

Some examples: a person who acts in a cowardly way, even though it is not against the law, has historically been deemed to be in the wrong by our society, and his cowardice is frowned upon; in our nation, we have always operated on the principle that we are responsible for our own decisions and actions, and we reject those who cannot accept responsibility for their conduct; a person who lies, which is not illegal except in a handful of cases, is ostracized by our society.

One of the reasons why morality is essential to self-government and the enjoyment of maximum liberty and freedom by the people is that those leaders chosen to govern normally reflect the population. If a people are a moral people, they will demand morality in their leaders. The reverse is also true. Immoral leaders are far less likely to enlarge the freedoms and liberties of the people.

The Founders understood the link between morality, virtue, and successful self-government. It was part of the unique and precious insight possessed by those who crafted the Constitution. The evidence of this insight and understanding is more than plentiful:

The oldest and most experienced of the Founders, Benjamin Franklin, summarized the understanding of the rest of the Founders, "Only a virtuous people are capable of freedom. As nations become corrupt and vicious, they have more need of masters."[2]

Unquestionably, the man who had prepared himself most thoroughly to influence the gathering that became the Constitutional Convention of 1787 was James Madison. He had studied history with the principal aim of understanding what had to be found in a democratic republic in order for it to survive and to thrive. He once made the observation, "Is there no virtue among us? If there be not, we are in a wretched situation. No theoretical checks—no form of government can render us secure. To suppose that any form of government will secure liberty or happiness without any virtue in the people, is a chimerical idea."[3]

Our nation's second President, John Adams, was a significant contributor to the Constitution although he was not a participant at the Constitutional Convention because he was serving as our nation's ambassador to Great Britain. He had crafted the new Constitution for the state of Massachusetts, which served as a model for the federal Constitution. He observed, "We have no government armed with power capable of contending with human passions unbridled by morality and religion. Avarice, ambition, revenge or gallantry, would break the strongest cords of our Constitution as a whale goes through a net. Our Constitution was made only for a moral and religious people. It is wholly inadequate to the government of any other."[4]

Finally, George Washington, in his salient farewell address to the nation, stated: "Of all the dispositions and habits which lead to political prosperity, religion and morality are indispensable supports. . . . It is substantially true that virtue or morality is a necessary spring of popular government. The rule, indeed, extends with more or less force to every species of free government."[5]

It is important to understand that those who founded this nation, who crafted the Constitution to govern it, knew not just that it could govern only a moral and virtuous people but that there was a clear link between morality, virtue, and religion.

The father of our nation, George Washington, understood that connection: "And let us with caution indulge the supposition that morality can be maintained without religion."[6]

In a letter to his friend, Thomas Jefferson, John Adams noted, "Without religion this world would be something not fit to be mentioned in polite company, I mean Hell."[7]

In another letter, this to his Philadelphia friend Benjamin Rush, Adams said, "Religion I hold to be essential to morals."[8]

One of the Founders who was tainted with scandal, found himself at odds with many of his contemporaries, and was ultimately the victim of a duel that went bad, Alexander Hamilton, still understood the basic truth, "Morality must fall without religion."[9]

The father of the Constitution, James Madison, noted, "Belief in a God All Powerful wise and good is so essential to the moral order of the world and to the happiness of man that arguments which enforce it cannot be drawn from too many sources."[10]

Thomas Jefferson, a skeptic of many of the religions of his age, still understood the connection between religion and the morality and virtue required by the nation he had helped create: "Reading, reflection and time have convinced me that the interests of society require the observation of those moral precepts . . . in which all religions agree."[11]

Whether one personally agrees with the assertion that morality and virtue are dependent upon religion is subjective. What cannot be disputed, however, is that the Founders of this nation firmly believed in the linkage between the two.

AMERICA'S PUBLIC RELIGION

Benjamin Franklin, like many of the Founders, was not a churchgoing Christian. Yet, as early as 1749 he referenced what he called America's "Public Religion." As believed by the Founders as a whole, that religious creed held to six basic tenets:

That there is a God, a creator,

That God created men equal under the law,

That He endowed mankind with certain inalienable rights,

That God is interested in the affairs of men,

That He rewards and punishes both nations and people,

That He is interested specifically in the United States of America.[12]

Evidence of the first three tenets of this Public Religion can be found in the Declaration of Independence, in the first lines of the second paragraph, "We hold these truths to be self-evident, that all men are created equal, that they are endowed by their Creator with certain inalienable Rights, that among these are Life, Liberty, and the pursuit of Happiness."[13]

The remaining three tenets are revealed in the writings of the Founders. For example, George Washington, in reflecting on the protection and assistance afforded the rebels in the early days of the American Revolution, said, "The Hand of Providence has been so conspicuous in all this, that he must be worse than an infidel that lacks faith, and more than wicked, that has not gratitude enough to acknowledge his obligations."[14]

James Madison, following an acknowledgment of the miraculous way in which the Constitution had come together, said, "It is impossible for any man of candor to reflect on this circumstance without partaking of the astonishment. It is impossible for the man of pious reflection not to perceive in it a finger of that Almighty hand which has been so frequently and signally extended to our relief in the critical stages of the revolution."[15]

Or consider the discourse offered by Benjamin Franklin at the critical moment in the Constitutional Convention of 1787:

In this situation of this assembly, groping, as it were, in the dark, to find political truth, and scarce able to distinguish it when presented to us, how has it happened, sir, that we have not hitherto once thought of humbly applying to the father of lights to illuminate our understandings? In the beginning of the contest with Britain, when we were sensible of danger, we had daily prayers in this room for the divine protection! Our prayers, sir, were heard; and they were graciously answered. All of us who were engaged in the struggle must have observed frequent instances of a superintending providence in our favor. I have lived, sir, a long time: and the longer I live, the more convincing proofs I see of this truth, that God governs in the affairs of men! And if a sparrow cannot fall to the ground without his notice, is it probable that an empire can rise without his aid?[16]

This Public Religion was so thoroughly ingrained in the minds of the Founders that they always, without hesitation, called upon God for His aid and thanked Him for His delivery and blessings.

It is why George Washington ended his first presidential oath by ad-libbing the words "So help me, God" and kissed the Bible upon which his hand had lain. It is why Thomas Jefferson, in his second inaugural address, asked God to give him enlightenment and inspiration.

It is why they prayed at the First Continental Congress, and in Congress ever since.

It is why Thomas Jefferson and Benjamin Franklin both proposed a seal for the new United States of America with biblical imagery. It is why the final seal approved has the "Eye of Providence" on it and the motto *Annuit Coeptis* ("God, or Providence, has favored our undertakings.")

It is why such a great President as Abraham Lincoln could refer to the people of the United States as God's "almost chosen people"—referring to God's purpose in raising up the United States to bring liberty to the world.[17]

It is why every one of our American Presidents has mentioned God in one euphemistic form or another in their inaugural address. For example,

George Washington spoke of the "benign Parent of the Human Race," James Madison of "that Almighty Being whose power regulates the destiny of nations," and Thomas Jefferson "that Infinite Power which rules the destinies of the universe." Teddy Roosevelt had his own unique literary term for God, the "Giver of Good." In each case, the role of deity in blessing our nation, or being invoked to do so, was a significant part of the President's address to the nation.[18]

THE FIRST AMENDMENT TO THE CONSTITUTION

In light of the Founders' foreknowledge that morality, virtue, and religion were indispensable to the success of their unique experiment in self-government, it is fair to inquire: What actions did they take to assure that morality, virtue, and religion were a part of the new American experience?

They did not hesitate to make these traits the highest priority. That is why the very first protection afforded the people of the United States, in the very first amendment to the Constitution, says "Congress shall make no law respecting an establishment of religion, or prohibiting the free exercise thereof."[19]

During the process of the ratification of the Constitution, a large number of its opponents, as well as many who supported it with some hesitation, argued that without a Bill of Rights, tyranny was possible. They wanted a clear statement of those individual rights that the citizens of the country had not surrendered to the new national government in agreeing to be governed by the Constitution.

Following the ratification of the Constitution, James Madison took it upon himself to satisfy the demands of those skeptics. He did so even though he did not think it was necessary—for he, along with many others, felt that because the national government had only the powers enumerated in the Constitution, and there was no mention of religion or the regulation of religion enumerated, the national government posed no threat to religion in the new nation.

In the first Congress, Madison proposed those amendments to the

Constitution that have become known as the Bill of Rights. The first of those amendments, as drafted by Madison, stated, "The civil rights of none shall be abridged on account of religious belief or worship, nor shall any national religion be established, nor shall the full and equal rights of conscience be in any manner, or on any pretext, infringed." By this language, Madison initiated the precedent of a two-pronged protection of religious liberty: one dealing with the establishment of a religion, and the second allowing the free exercise of religion without the national government interfering. The second protection is usually referred to as the "free exercise" language. Our discussion will focus on the first, what is usually referred to as the "establishment" language.

Clearly, by the language Madison proposed, he only sought to prevent the creation, and presumably the support through taxation, of a national religion. He wanted to avoid that which then existed in a number of the states—state-supported religions.

Throughout the debate that followed, this narrow view of what Madison and the Congress were seeking is consistent with the arguments made in support of the amendment. Madison stated in the course of that debate, for example, "that he apprehended the meaning of the words to be, that Congress should not establish a religion, and enforce the legal observation of it by law, nor compel men to worship God in any manner contrary to their conscience."

Later in the debate, the proposed language was altered to say, "no religion shall be established by law." In response, Madison offered an amendment to include the word "national" before "religion."

Ultimately, the language was revised significantly to that wording ratified by the states and found in the Constitution today.

It is significant that Madison's view on what the establishment wording of the First Amendment intended was very narrow—no national religion. There was nothing spoken or offered by James Madison, or any of the other members of that first Congress, suggesting that what was being sought was a wall between the government and religion. There was nothing to suggest that what was desired was a government that was absolutely neutral when it came to religion. There was nothing more than an expressed desire that there never be a national church or a government that supported one religious sect over another.

Did those who drafted, debated, passed, and ratified the First Amendment to the Constitution want a wall between the government and religion? Did they expect the government to stay entirely out of religion? Did they expect the government to be entirely neutral when it came to religion?

The answer to these questions is best found in the actions of that first Congress and those that immediately followed.

The day after the House of Representatives adopted the religion clauses in the First Amendment, a resolution was offered requesting that President Washington issue a Thanksgiving Day Proclamation thanking God for the many blessings poured out on the new nation. The resolution passed, and within two weeks George Washington issued that proclamation in which he set aside a day in November for the people to offer sincere thanks for God's protection, His care, and His mercies during the Revolutionary War, and to humbly beseech His forgiveness for both national and other transgressions.

Subsequently, Presidents John Adams and James Madison issued similar Thanksgiving Proclamations. Thomas Jefferson did not because he did not believe it was for the government to dictate the times of fasting and what the people were to say in their personal prayers.

That same Congress, simultaneously with its consideration of the First Amendment, debated and enacted the Northwest Ordinance. That law provided for the governance of the "Northwest Territories"—that area that was to become the states of Ohio, Indiana, Illinois, Michigan, Wisconsin, and Minnesota. That ordinance stated that "religion, morality and knowledge, being necessary to good government and the happiness of mankind, schools and the means of education shall forever be encouraged."[20] Accordingly, grants of tax dollars for schools were provided for, including grants to religious schools.

Similar grants for religious schools were included in subsequent acts of Congress. For example, President Thomas Jefferson's 1803 treaty with the Kaskaskia Indians included a requirement that the government of the United States provide cash support for the tribe's Roman Catholic priest and school:

> And whereas, The greater part of the said tribe have been baptised and received into the Catholic church to which they are much attached, the United States will give annually for seven years one hundred dollars towards the support of a priest of that religion, who will engage to perform for the said tribe the duties of his office and also to instruct as many of their children as possible in the rudiments of literature. And the United States will further give the sum of three hundred dollars to assist the said tribe in the erection of a church.[21]

Similar grants for religious organizations to provide education for Native Americans were to continue for nearly a hundred years, until 1897.

If their actions are not sufficient evidence, perhaps the expressed words of the earliest, closest in time to, and most respected Constitutional authority might be convincing.

Next to *The Federalist,* the source most often quoted in Court decisions for the Founders' intentions regarding the Constitution is Joseph Story's *Commentaries on the Constitution of the United States.* Story was a member of the Supreme Court from 1811 to 1845. He was also a professor at Harvard Law School for much of that time. In his *Commentaries* he stated that the First Amendment was universally understood to allow the government of the United States to encourage Christianity as long as the actions taken did not interfere with the private rights of conscience and the freedom to worship. He further said that if the First Amendment had been used to attempt to level all religions, or to be indifferent to religion, it would have resulted in "universal indignation" among the American people.[22]

What the American people at the time believed is very relevant to understanding what those who crafted the Constitution intended. It was the people themselves, "We the People," to whom the Constitution was turned over for ratification. The delegates to the Constitutional Convention purposely did not look to the Congress for approval of their product; they demanded that the people elect members to state ratifying conventions to either adopt or reject the Constitution.

That understanding of the people is clearly reflected in the state constitutions that were being adopted contemporaneously by the people of the new states. For example, the 1780 Massachusetts State Constitution permitted liberty of religious conscience, but it imposed taxes on the citizens to support churches and Protestant teachers. The reason given: "As the happiness of a people and the good order and preservation of civil government essentially depend upon piety, religion, and morality, and as these cannot be generally diffused through a community but by the institution of the public worship of God and of public instructions in piety, religion, and morality . . ."[23]

This syllogism—republican government requires a virtuous citizenry; the cultivation of virtue depends on religion; therefore, supporters of republican government ought to support religion—dominated the thinking of every state. Three other states accomplished that goal by allowing public support of religion. Six additional states sought to accomplish that goal by requiring a religious test. For example, Pennsylvania did not support religion with taxation, but its Constitution adopted in 1776 required that each member of its House of Representatives declare a belief in one God and that the Old and New Testaments were given by divine inspiration.

Virginia, Rhode Island, and New York took an entirely different approach. At the urging of James Madison and Thomas Jefferson, Virginia abolished its state-supported religion and passed "A Bill Establishing Religious Freedom." This act stated that liberty of conscience was one of those natural rights endowed by the Creator upon man and that it cannot be taken by the government. It eliminated tax support for religion and prohibited government from compelling any person to worship or not to worship.

Of great importance, however, is the fact that Virginia, and those two states that agreed with its approach, did so only because they believed that religion did better without government assistance or interference. Madison, who fought for the bill in the Virginia legislature, sincerely believed that the religiously produced moral character demanded of the citizens of the nation he helped to create would come about in greater purity without government aid.[24]

But Madison also believed that the issue of whether states should or should not support religion with tax dollars was entirely a matter for the states. It is also clear that those who supported the First Amendment's establishment language were fully intending to keep the national government out of that debate, clarifying that the national government had no role in determining what the states did on the issue.

There can be very little argument about what was intended by those who wrote and ratified the First Amendment to the Constitution—simply, it meant no national church and no government preference among religious sects. It did not mean indifference and most assuredly not antagonism.[25]

This understanding of what was intended by the establishment language was so clearly comprehended that the Founders had no hesitance in opening up the newly constructed home of the House of Representatives for the conducting of religious services each Sunday. Further, Presidents Thomas Jefferson and James Madison apparently felt no discomfort or fear that they were violating the First Amendment to the Constitution as they sat and worshipped in a makeshift pew in the primary home of government, Sabbath after Sabbath.[26]

POLYGAMY AND THE WALL

For the next 150 years, the citizens and government of the United States, as well as the citizens and governments of the various states, operated as they understood the Constitution. Governments, both state and federal, were very friendly to religion. During those years, there was considerable intermingling of government and religious institutions and practices. Examples include the funding of religious schools by both the federal and state governments, prayers offered in classes and school activities, Bible reading at the start of the school day, religion being taught alongside secular subjects, subsidized transportation of parochial school students, nativity scenes in the town square, Ten Commandment monuments erected on government property, chaplains in the military, prayers to open Congressional sessions and state legislatures, proclamations offered by Presidents and governors calling on the people to thank God, repeated references to the tenets of the Public Religion by Presidents and innumerable other elected officials, embracing of a national anthem referencing God, and a national motto, "In God We Trust," on our currency.

During that 150-year period, no one went to court asserting that the Constitution was being violated. There were no Supreme Court decisions in which the establishment clause was raised as a challenge to these practices. This intermingling was accepted as normal and desirable by everyone, including the United States Supreme Court. In an 1892 opinion, the Supreme Court noted the multitude of evidence that would justify it in declaring, "This is a religious nation, . . . this is a Christian nation."[27]

There was one Supreme Court opinion of note during that period in which the Court interpreted the religion language of the First Amendment. That case involved the free exercise language of the First Amendment, but it became the case upon which the Supreme Court was ultimately to rely in providing a novel interpretation of the establishment language.

The case was *Reynolds v. United States*.[28] George Reynolds was a member of The Church of Jesus Christ of Latter-day Saints, often referred to as the Mormon church, and a practicing polygamist. Utah was then a territory of the United States and thus subject to Congress. Congress had outlawed bigamy, and Reynolds became the test case for the constitutionality of that law. At his criminal trial, Reynolds argued that under the free exercise language of the First Amendment, he was entitled to practice the religious belief of polygamy as preached by his church.

The Supreme Court ruled that the First Amendment free exercise language protected only opinions and beliefs and not actions. Thus, Congress can outlaw certain religious practices. The Court's opinion relied in part on the language from a letter written by Thomas Jefferson to the Danbury Baptist Association in 1802. In that letter, Jefferson used the metaphor that the amendment was intended to build a "wall of separation between church and State."

Ultimately, this metaphor was to replace the constitutional language itself.

DISGRUNTLED TAXPAYER—ARCH R. EVERSON

In 1941, the state of New Jersey passed a law that sanctioned the use of state funds to underwrite bus transportation for school-age students. The legislation specifically allowed subsidization of the transportation of students attending parochial schools. The law followed a pattern that at least sixteen other states had established.

Ewing Township was a rural area of New Jersey, and many of its students had to travel long distances to attend their schools. Its board of education passed a resolution authorizing reimbursement to the parents of students for the costs of taking public transportation. The resolution covered those attending Catholic schools as well as public schools. The amount allocated for reimbursing the transportation costs of students going to Catholic schools was small, less than $400.

Arch R. Everson was a local taxpayer and a member of a national organization that was committed to ending taxpayer support for parochial schools. He was selected to be the plaintiff in the lawsuit to challenge the resolution passed by the Ewing Township Board of Education. He presented himself as a taxpayer within the school district and the vice president of a state taxpayers association and sued the Ewing Township Board of Education.

The Supreme Court had previously ruled that the First Amendment to the Constitution was applicable to the states under the Fourteenth Amendment. The specific question to be decided by the Court in Arch Everson's case was whether the use of New Jersey tax dollars to subsidize the transportation of students to Catholic schools was a law respecting the establishment of religion.

The majority opinion, written by Justice Hugo Black, included a recital of the history of abuse by different religious majorities in the pre-Revolutionary War era of American history. He contended that this resulted in the demand for the protection of religious liberty in the Constitution.

Black focused on the efforts of James Madison and Thomas Jefferson to pass the Virginia Bill for Religious Liberty in 1785–1786. He asserted that the motivation of Jefferson and Madison in seeking passage of the Virginia law was what had motivated Madison when he sought Congressional approval of the religious liberty language of the First Amendment three years later.

In making this argument, Justice Black took certain liberties. For example, he claimed that the Supreme Court had previously found that the First Amendment had the same objective as the Virginia statute. He cited three prior Supreme Court decisions to justify that conclusion. An examination of those three opinions shows that they do not stand for that proposition at all. None of them reach that conclusion; two of the opinions do not even mention the Virginia statute.[29]

Justice Black further claimed that Thomas Jefferson played a leading role in the drafting and adoption of the First Amendment, failing to acknowledge that Jefferson was not even in the country during those months of 1789—he was serving as our nation's ambassador to France.

Finally, Justice Black did not review the proceedings of Congress in debating and passing the First Amendment. He had no knowledge of what James Madison had proposed as the original language or what he said in the subsequent debates. Black did not review that record until after *Everson* had been decided.[30]

Following his discussion of the Virginia legislation, Black's opinion stated the following:

The 'establishment of religion' clause of the First Amendment means at least this: Neither a state nor the Federal Government can set up a church. Neither can pass laws which aid one religion, aid all religions, or prefer one religion over another. Neither can force nor influence a person to go to or to remain away from church against his will or force him to profess a belief or disbelief in any religion. No person can be punished for entertaining or professing religious beliefs or disbeliefs, for church attendance or non-attendance. No tax in any amount, large or small, can be levied to support any religious activities or institutions, whatever they may be called, or whatever form they may adopt to teach or practice religion. Neither a state nor the Federal Government can, openly or secretly, participate in the affairs of any religious organization or groups and vice versa. *In the words of Jefferson, the clause against establishment of religion by law was intended to erect "a wall of separation between Church and State."*[31]

Interestingly, those words parrot a passage from a book written by Charles Beard, a notable and controversial historian of the first half of the twentieth century who had written a tome in which he argued that the Founders were motivated by economics, specifically the protection of their own wealth, and not by a noble philosophy.[32]

Later in the opinion, Justice Black said that "The First Amendment has erected a wall between church and state. That wall must be kept high and impregnable. We could not approve the slightest breach."[33]

Ironically, the majority of five concluded that the wall had not been breached in the case of the New Jersey statute or the resolution of the Township of Ewing. Four Justices dissented, finding that it had been breached and the law should have been declared unconstitutional.

The state of New Jersey may have won the battle, but Arch R. Everson won the war. The use of the metaphor "wall of separation between church and state" now took on a life of its own.[34]

> IS OUR NATION TRULY BETTER OFF
> WHEN ONLY PRIVATE EXPRESSIONS OF
> RELIGION ARE ACCEPTABLE?

THE WALL THAT HUGO BUILT

A year later, in the case of *McCollum v. Board of Education*,[35] the wall metaphor received new prominence when it was used to terminate a voluntary program in Champaign County, Illinois. In 1940, members of the Jewish, Catholic, and several Protestant faiths created an association called the Champaign Council on Religious Education. The council received permission from the board of education to offer classes in religious instruction to students in grades four through nine. Students had to submit a signed permission slip from their parents to attend a 30- to 45-minute class on religious instruction weekly. The instructors were provided and paid for by the members of the council. The classes took place in the school classrooms.

In an opinion again penned by Justice Black, the Supreme Court found the practice violated the establishment language of the First Amendment. "The majority in the *Everson* case . . . agreed that the First Amendment's language, properly interpreted, had erected a wall of separation between Church and State."[36] The majority opinion rejected the school board's argument that the First Amendment only prevented the government from showing a preference for one religion over another, not, as in this case, a situation in which the government provided impartial assistance to all religions.

The decision was not unanimous. In Justice Stanley Reed's dissent, he pointed out that Thomas Jefferson, as the rector of the University of Virginia (the university he founded as a state institution), not only encouraged but expected the university's students to participate in religious classes. James Madison was a member of the board of visitors that approved that policy. (The rector and visitors are the equivalent of the board of trustees of the university.)

Reed's point was that if Jefferson had truly wanted a wall erected between church and state, he would not have permitted the exclusion of that wall at his own university.

Reed's argument that "[a] rule of law should not be drawn from a figure of speech" was not convincing to the other members of the Court.[37] But, in fact, the figure of speech had supplanted the language of the Constitution itself.

Soon, state courts began to rely on *Everson* to axe interconnected church and government practices. In 1948, the supreme court of New Mexico brought an end to a practice whereby a number of local school districts had relied on Catholic schools to provide the education needs of public school students. The practice had been instituted in eleven counties in New Mexico and involved more than thirty schools. The case was watched with great interest at the national level. In the end, the New Mexico Supreme Court found the practice to violate the *Everson* standard.[38]

Prayers in schools were targeted by the Supreme Court in the 1962 case of *Engel v. Vitale.*[39] At issue was the participation of students in the state of New York in daily reciting a prayer written by the state's board of regents. The board had implemented the practice and drafted the prayer to avoid the possibility of running afoul of *Everson.* Students who did not wish to recite the prayer or to hear it recited were allowed to leave the classroom. The wording of the prayer, generic as it could be, read: "Almighty God, we acknowledge our dependence upon Thee, and beg Thy blessings upon us, our teachers, and our country." The Court, in an opinion written by Justice Black, declared the practice to be equivalent to the establishment of an official religion, and it was declared unconstitutional. Only one Justice dissented.

Subsequently, the Court outlawed a moment of silence in public schools, clergy-led prayers at graduation ceremonies, and eventually student-led prayers at football games.

One year after *Engel,* the target was Bible reading in public schools. The states of Pennsylvania and Maryland had requirements that some

Bible verses or chapters be read daily. Students could be excused if their parents requested such in writing. Pennsylvania had required the reading since 1928 and Maryland since 1905. The Supreme Court declared both state laws to be in violation of the First Amendment in the case of *Abington School District v. Schempp*.[40] Citing *Everson,* the majority opinion made the rather questionable statement that the views of Jefferson and Madison came to be incorporated, not only in the federal Constitution, but in those of most of the states. That statement ignored the fact that at the time of the adoption of the Constitution, four states had tax-supported religions and six more had religious tests for holding public office. The Court, relying on *Everson,* again denied the argument made by the states that the purpose of the First Amendment was only to prohibit the government from preferring one religion over another.

In his sole dissent, Justice Potter Stewart criticized the notion that the language of the First Amendment, both the establishment language and the free exercise language, had somehow been reduced to the simplified "separation of church and state." He bemoaned the idea that such a standard could be applied mechanically in a nation where religion and government had interacted in countless ways throughout our nation's history. He referred to the wall of separation as a "sterile metaphor."

Stewart also identified what many in our nation, as far back as 1963, were seeing occur:

> For a compulsory state educational system so structures a child's life that if religious exercises are held to be an impermissible activity in schools, religion is placed at an artificial and state-created disadvantage. Viewed in this light, permission of such exercises for those who want them is necessary if the schools are truly to be neutral in the matter of religion. *And a refusal to permit religious exercises thus is seen, not as the realization of state neutrality, but rather as the establishment of a religion of secularism, or at the least, as government support of the beliefs of those who think that religious exercises should be conducted only in private.*[41]

Many more such decisions were to follow.

In the first 150 years of our nation's history, the Supreme Court had but a handful of cases in which it was called upon to give meaning to the religion clauses of the First Amendment. Since it opened the door with its *Everson* ruling in 1947, it has been inundated with petitions to decide what does and does not constitute a breach of the wall of separation.

The Court has handed down more than forty decisions attempting to define what is and what is not an appropriate interaction between religion and government under the establishment language. Many more cases have been decided based on the free exercise language. In those various decisions, the Court has waffled badly. It has found, for example, that a nativity scene sponsored by the government is unconstitutional, but a Hanukkah menorah is not. It has found it very difficult to decide when a display of the Ten Commandments on government property is breaching the wall of separation. It has decided that a state may lend geography textbooks that contain maps of the United States to parochial school children, but the state may not lend maps of the United States alone. It has concluded that the government can lend textbooks on colonial U.S. history, but not a film on George Washington along with a film projector.

The Court has decided that a state can give money to a parochial school to reimburse the school for conducting state-mandated tests, but it cannot provide funds for parochial-school teachers to give teacher-prepared tests on secular subjects. Exceptional parochial students may receive counseling funded by the state, but the counseling must take place somewhere other than in the parochial school—in a trailer parked down the street, for example.[42]

THE FUTURE?

In the 1952 case of *Zorach v. Clauson,* the Supreme Court acknowledged that "We are a religious people whose institutions presuppose a Supreme Being."[43] A nation that is, by its history and form of government, a religious nation now finds itself ever struggling to establish the proper

14. Spalding, *Founders' Almanac,* 148.

15. Hamilton, Jay, and Madison, *The Federalist,* 193.

16. Meacham, *American Gospel,* 88–89.

17. Wolf, *Almost Chosen People,* 13.

18. See Bellah, "Civil Religion in America."

19. Constitution of the United States, Bill of Rights; accessed online at https://www.ourdocuments.gov/doc.php?doc=13&page=transcript.

20. Northwest Ordinance, 1787; accessed online at https://www.ourdocuments.gov/doc.php?doc=8&page=transcript.

21. Accessed online at http://digital.library.okstate.edu/kappler/vol2/treaties/kas0067.htm#mn5.

22. Story, *Commentaries,* 700.

23. Munoz, "Original Meaning," 606.

24. For a full discussion of the approaches of the states to the issue of religion and morality, see ibid.

25. See the dissenting opinion of Justice William Rehnquist in the case of *Wallace v. Jaffree,* 472 U.S. 38 (1985) for the source of this information concerning the Founders' intent and early actions and opinions as to the meaning of the establishment language of the First Amendment.

26. Library of Congress. "Religion and the Federal Government, Part 2," accessed online at http://www.loc.gov/exhibits/religion/rel06-2.html.

27. *Rector, etc. of Holy Trinity Church v. United States,* 143 U.S. 457, 470–471 (1892).

28. *Reynolds v. United States,* 98 U.S. 145 (1878).

29. Munoz, "Original Meaning," 589.

30. Newman, *Hugo Black,* 365.

31. *Everson v. Board of Education,* 330 U.S. 1, 15–16 (1947); emphasis added.

32. Newman, *Hugo Black,* 363. See also Beard, *The Republic,* 165. Beard is the author of *An Economic Interpretation of the Constitution of the United States,* in which he argues that the Founders were part of an elite class who brought about the Constitution to further their economic well-being. His scholarship has been widely panned in recent decades.

33. *Everson v. Board of Education,* 330 U.S. 1, 18 (1947).

34. See generally *Everson v. Board of Education,* 330 U.S. 1 (1947).

35. *McCollum v. Board of Education,* 333 U.S. 203 (1948).

36. Ibid., 211.

37. Ibid., 247.

38. See *Zellers v. Huff,* 236 P.2d 949 (1951).

39. *Engel v. Vitale,* 370 U.S. 421 (1962).

40. *School District of Abington Township v. Schempp,* 374 U.S. 203 (1963).

41. Ibid., 313; emphasis added.

42. See Justice Rehnquist's dissent in *Wallace v. Jaffree,* 472 U.S. 38 (1985) and Rossum and Tarr, *American Constitutional Law,* 223–79, for these and other examples.

43. *Zorach v. Clauson,* 343 U.S. 306, 313 (1952).

HOW THE SUPREME COURT EMPOWERED FEDERAL JUDGES TO RAISE TAXES, MANAGE SCHOOL DISTRICTS, AND GENERALLY WORK THEIR WILL

MISSOURI V. JENKINS (1990)

"The accumulation of all powers, legislative, executive, and judiciary, in the same hands, whether of one, a few, or many, . . . may justly be pronounced the very definition of tyranny."

—*James Madison*

THE FOUNDERS AND THE JUDGES

The Founders of this nation feared tyranny. They saw the checks on each of the three independent and coequal branches of government as a crucial restraint on the ability of any single branch to become supreme and independently all-powerful. It was believed that each branch would jealously guard its own privileges and power and, in the course of doing so, keep the other two in check.

Vesting an excess of power in the least accountable of the three branches, the judiciary, would never have been acceptable to the Founders. Because of the independence that members of the federal judiciary possess, they truly are unaccountable. The Constitution prohibits their salaries from being reduced. The Constitution also affords federal judges lifetime appointments "during good behavior." They can be removed from office only by being impeached and convicted by the Congress. In the more-than-225-year history of the United States, there have been only eight federal judges impeached by the House of Representatives, convicted by the Senate, and removed from office.[1]

In an effort to convince the people of New York to ratify the Constitution, Alexander Hamilton argued that the judiciary would always be the least dangerous of the three branches because it did not control either the "sword," meaning executive powers, including military and law enforcement, or the "purse," the ability to raise and spend money. "The judiciary has no influence over either the sword or the purse, no direction either of the strength or of the wealth of the society; and can take no active resolution whatever."

He argued that because the three branches were separate and independent, the only way the judicial branch could pose a threat to the rights of the people would be if it were joined by another branch in that threat: "It equally proves, that though individual oppression may now and then proceed from the courts of justice, the general liberty of the people can never be endangered from that quarter; I mean so long as the judiciary remains truly distinct from both the legislature and the Executive."[2]

Hamilton's primary argument to those who opposed the Constitution was always that the judiciary did not possess the ability to force its will on the people, only the ability to exercise judgment in interpreting the law.

It is important to remember that the Constitution assigns to the legislative branch the power to raise taxes. More specifically, it entrusts that power to the House of Representatives. Why? Because a people who were motivated to revolt by the battle cry, "No taxation without representation!" wanted to make certain that it was the House of Representatives, whose members faced the electorate every two years, that controlled the purse (spending) and the power to impose taxes.

The thought that a single judge would ever possess the ability to raise taxes and to spend those taxes independent of any meaningful oversight—in effect combining the judicial, legislative, and executive powers in one individual—would have sent a dagger to the heart of any member of the founding generation.

But when faced with a perceived need to end our nation's shameful era of school segregation, that is just what happened in the case of *Missouri v. Jenkins.*

THE NATION PURSUES INTEGRATION

The beginning of the end of America's sad chapter of government-mandated segregation was triggered by the Supreme Court's decision in *Brown v. Board of Education* in 1954, which effectively reversed *Plessy v. Ferguson.* Although *Plessy* had to do with segregated cars on railroads and *Brown* dealt with segregated public schools, the latter set in motion a series of decisions by the courts that declared "separate but equal" unconstitutional across the board.

The Court's decision in *Brown v. Board of Education* was quite short and precise. The Supreme Court held that separate is inherently unequal. More precisely, based upon studies showing that segregation in public schooling inflicted lasting feelings of inferiority on African-American children, the Court held that segregated education was inherently unequal and thus unconstitutional.

But with that declaration, segregation in schools did not suddenly disappear—to the contrary. The *Brown* decision did not provide any remedy or timetable. It was not until the next year, in a case entitled *Brown II,* that the Court ordered that desegregation was to end "with all deliberate speed." This phrase had little precision to it. In *Brown II,* federal district court judges were vested by the Supreme Court with the equitable power and wide discretion to choose timetables, to shape solutions, and to find remedies to end segregation. They were to exercise that oversight until the school district had achieved the goal of desegregation—although that term was not defined.

Despite the fact that the federal district court judges were vested with this immense power, in the next decade it was exercised very little. There simply were not many lawsuits filed challenging segregated schools.

This was remarkable because most of the Southern states resisted the effort to desegregate public schools. When the original *Brown* decision was made in 1954, only .001 percent of black students in the South and border South were attending schools with white students. In the next ten years that figure had risen only to 2.3 percent.

The passage of the Civil Rights Act of 1964 generated new activity in the courts. That federal legislation gave the Justice Department the power to sue school districts and states to achieve desegregation. It also provided financial support for private efforts to bring lawsuits.

Suddenly, the courts were back in charge of the effort to end segregation in public schools. Many more lawsuits were filed.

By 1968, the percentage of black students attending schools with whites in the Southern and border South states increased to 32 percent.

One of the means by which Southern states addressed segregation was by implementing "freedom of choice" remedies, which called for public-school-aged children to attend the neighborhood school of their choice. Such programs took on the appearance of ending segregated schools, but in most instances, that was only an appearance, not a reality.

In 1968, the Supreme Court said that "freedom of choice" was insufficient in the case of the schools in New Kent County, Virginia. The Court ruled, in effect, that desegregation by allowing choice of schools was not working in the case of the New Kent County schools, and it ordered the district to implement a plan that integrated the schools.

This was a significant shift in what the Supreme Court deemed to be acceptable. Simply ending "separate but equal" was no longer enough. Allowing black students to attend schools of their choice was insufficient. Thereafter, *integration*, not just the end of segregation, became the unstated objective of the Supreme Court.

Federal district courts were told to utilize their equitable powers to order and/or approve plans to bring about integration of the nation's school systems. In the ensuing years, hundreds of school districts around the country came under the supervision of federal judges. That supervision would last for years, even decades, in some cases.

It paid off. Between 1968 and 1970, the percentage of black students attending schools with white students went from 32 percent to almost 86 percent in the Southern and border South states.

Three years later, the Supreme Court endorsed the busing of students to speed up the integration of public schools. With court-ordered busing, a certain number of students from one part of a school district were not allowed to attend their local school, but were forced to take a bus to another part of the school district to attend a school in order to achieve integration. This decision was important not just because it endorsed the use of busing to desegregate schools, but because the Court's rationale justified an even broader and more extensive authority in the federal district courts. In effect, the Supreme Court said there was no limit to the remedies a court could order using its equitable powers.

By 1972, over 91 percent of black students were enrolled in schools with white students.

Busing, however, became very controversial. Parents of both white and black students were upset to have their children hauled to schools far removed from their neighborhoods. It angered them to see their young children forced to take long bus rides when there might be a school just walking distance away. This opposition sometimes became very intense. Parents in some communities rioted or engaged in acts of civil disobedience such as lying down in front of school buses in an effort to thwart court-ordered busing.

One of the side effects of aggressive, court-ordered remedies to integrate schools, such as court-ordered busing, was "white flight." During the period after World War II, the movement of white families from urban areas to the suburbs had become somewhat common. It exploded, however, once the courts began to order integration measures such as busing. The unfortunate result was fewer and fewer white students in the urban schools. This greatly complicated the efforts to integrate schools. It became common for urban schools to be largely black and suburban schools primarily white.

Detroit was one of those cities where white flight had created areas of black-only and white-only neighborhoods. The net effect was the reality of segregated urban-suburban schools. To achieve the integration that the district court believed was required by the Supreme Court, a federal judge ordered a solution that not only called for busing of students within the Detroit School District but also incorporated fifty-three suburban school districts into the busing scheme.

At this juncture, 1974, the Supreme Court drew a line when it came to the power of district court judges to order integration. The Court found that court-ordered busing between school districts was not permitted unless there was evidence that it was the result of conscious government action. The Court also emphasized that local control of schools could not be ignored.

With this decision, judges and school districts had to turn to new and innovative ways to address segregation where urban school districts were overwhelmingly black and surrounding suburban districts were overwhelmingly white. One innovative experiment was the creation of magnet schools, schools with unique and special programs that would lure white students from the suburbs to attend urban schools. The theory was that such schools would offer educational opportunities so attractive that suburban students would make the effort and overcome the hesitance to attend urban schools.

It is important to understand that in the decades after *Brown,* federal district courts all over the nation engaged in crafting integration plans or ordered local school districts to come up with their own plans for court approval. It would be wrong to think of segregated schools as a phenomenon exclusive to the South or border South states. Significant court decisions involving integration plans arose out of California, Colorado, and Massachusetts.

Thus, in the two decades following the Supreme Court's decision in *Brown v. Board of Education,* the parameters had been set. Desegregation was no longer the goal—it was now integration. District courts were authorized to exercise their full equitable powers to integrate school districts, imposing their own plans or approving plans generated by the school districts. Among the methods relied upon during this era included freedom of school choice, but only where such plans could show integration was occurring; court-ordered busing—but not over school district boundaries; use of "magnet schools"; other voluntary transfers (for example, students could transfer from any school where they were in the majority to a school where they would be in the minority); and assignment of students to specific neighborhood schools to achieve integration.[3]

THE HISTORY OF SEGREGATION IN MISSOURI

The history of the border area between the states of Missouri and Kansas, where Kansas City, Missouri, is located, is a storied history of conflict over slavery and race. When Kansas attempted to join the Union as a free state in the 1850s with no slavery allowed, its neighbor to the east rebelled. Missouri was a slave state, and its people wanted to force Kansas to be a slave state as well. The bloody days before the American Civil War, with Kansas Jayhawkers and Missouri Bushwhackers fighting for their respective causes, resulted in the name "Bleeding Kansas." Most of the bleeding occurred on the eastern side of Kansas and the western side of Missouri and was generated by slave owners in Missouri.

Missouri was the northernmost state to require segregated schools in its constitution. As late as 1948, Missouri had more than 6,000 school districts, but only about 300 offered a high school education for either white or black students. Most districts excluded blacks, especially those districts in rural Missouri. Simply put, educating black students was considered optional in most areas of the state. Still, separate but theoretically equal schools did exist prior to *Brown* in some urban areas of the state.

Over the years, Missouri was the source of a substantial amount of civil rights litigation. For example, Supreme Court decisions arising out of Missouri held that the state had to provide a separate but equal law school for black law students instead of paying the tuition of black law students to attend a law school in an adjoining state (1938); struck down restrictive covenants in housing that prohibited whites from selling property to blacks (1948); and applied federal law prohibiting discrimination in the private sales of housing (1968).

After *Brown,* the state of Missouri took some actions to comply with its mandate. Unlike many of the Southern and border South states, it did not belligerently resist the decision.

Still, it appeared to some that those supervising the Kansas City schools labored to assure that its schools remained segregated. School boundaries were drawn and redrawn, sometimes a block at a time, to keep black students assigned to majority black schools.

Real-estate lending practices of banks and marketing methods of real-estate agents in the decades after *Brown* worked to further segregate the races. Blacks were steered to certain neighborhoods by real-estate agents. Banks would redline certain neighborhoods and would not lend to black families in white areas.

White flight was common. Between 1958 and 1973, sixty thousand whites moved from the urban areas of Kansas City to the suburbs.

The effect on school populations was dramatic. At one high school in 1959, 6.6 percent of the students were black. Ten years later, black students made up 98 percent of the student body. At another high school, in 1955 the school had 1,533 white students and 195 black students. One decade later, only 16 white students attended the school.

By the mid-1970s, although whites remained the majority population in Kansas City, Missouri, the city's urban schools were mostly all black, with a few white schools on the outward fringe of the city.

Simultaneously, the school district finances were tanking. The last year that the student enrollment was mostly white, 1969, was the last year that the majority white population voted a levy increase or a bond measure to improve schools. In the years that followed, elections to increase funding for the school system failed nineteen times.

The fact that after 1969 no new levies or bonding were approved was arguably because of racism, but it was also attributable to the aging of the population generally, with fewer households with students. Kansas City also had a large number of private schools, and the parents of private school students had little incentive to support more taxes for the public schools.

Of considerable importance, the state of Missouri required that any local tax increase over a certain level be approved by a super-majority—two-thirds of the electorate. That level of support for a tax increase was an insurmountable hurdle.

In 1974 and again in 1977 teachers in the Kansas City School District (KCSD) went on strike. The strikes lasted multiple weeks, some of the teachers were jailed for disorderly conduct, and the relationship was poisoned between the teachers, the administration, and the public. After both strikes, the school district lost thousands of students, both white and black, to private schools and moves outside the district.

During the 1970s, the administration of the KCSD became infamous for incompetence and ineptitude. That ineptitude was shared by those elected to the school board. The fact that those responsible for running the schools were incapable of doing so in a skilled manner was a source of great frustration in the black community—those with the most students in the district and thus the most at risk.

This combination of challenges left the school district not only segregated but with deteriorating facilities. Bills were not being paid for months. The grass wasn't getting cut in the playgrounds. Carpets had to be repaired with duct tape. Asbestos fell from pipes, and windows fell out of windowpanes.

The children of the KCSD suffered the most. They were being denied a solid education. Doors of opportunity were being slammed in their faces. Advanced education and decent employment opportunities were being refused them.

The final affront was that the federal government investigated the school district, found it to be segregated, and demanded a plan to desegregate. Even though a majority of both white and black parents opposed busing, the school board was forced to adopt a busing plan to suit the federal bureaucrats. The busing plan diverted money into buses, money that was more desperately needed in the schoolhouses and classrooms.

In the first year that the busing plan was implemented, 21 percent of the district's remaining white students fled the district.

Something had to give.[4]

THE LAWSUIT

In desperation, in May of 1977, the Kansas City School District school board did something that had never been done before—it filed its own desegregation lawsuit. Previously, every desegregation lawsuit had been filed by a group of parents or a civil rights organization. The district knew that it could never satisfy the demands of the federal government because its minority population was too high. It had to find relief somewhere.

As the plaintiffs, the school board named as defendants the states of Missouri and Kansas and several departments of the federal government, alleging that they were all responsible for the racial makeup of the Kansas City School District because of the historical practices the defendants had each pursued.

The case was assigned to Judge Russell G. Clark, a new appointee to the federal bench. Judge Clark had been raised on a farm in rural southern Missouri and had attended a one-room schoolhouse. He served in World War II and, after the war, attended college and law school. Besides his practice as an attorney, he also had a long history of involvement in Missouri politics. President Jimmy Carter appointed Judge Clark at the request of Senator Thomas Eagleton. He was viewed as a moderate-to-conservative judge who would likely look for a modest solution to the KCSD's segregated schools. He was to show otherwise.

A year after the lawsuit was filed, a local attorney, Arthur Benson, took over as lead attorney for the plaintiffs. Benson had come from a background very different from those that he was to represent for years into the future. He had attended the best schools, and he enjoyed a fortunate lifestyle. Benson had become a staunch liberal in high school, and his practice of the law reflected his commitment to the underdog. He was to stay with the case for nearly two decades.

Benson and Clark developed a unique relationship. In the years that followed, Benson rarely lost any argument before Judge Clark.

A year after the lawsuit was filed by the school board, Judge Clark demonstrated that he was in control of the litigation. He issued an order in which the school board was dismissed as the plaintiff and realigned as a defendant. Thereafter, the plaintiffs were schoolchildren.

This move, odd as it seemed at the time, facilitated all that Clark ordered thereafter. With students as the plaintiffs and both the school board and the state of Missouri as defendants, a pathway was created for what Judge Clark was to determine was the reasonable solution to the segregated KCSD.

Arthur Benson took years to prepare for the trial necessary to establish the facts. By the time the case finally came before Judge Clark in late 1983, the school district had seen the student population decline by almost 50 percent from when the lawsuit was commenced in the mid-1970s. The percentage of students that were black had risen to almost 68 percent from the 60 percent figure in 1977.

To most, this was proof of the incompetence of the school district more than racism. Arthur Benson, however, claimed it was evidence of the racial animus of those fleeing the urban area, resulting in a less diverse school population and denied funding. This was the essence of the case he presented to Judge Clark.

The trial was unique in that the plaintiffs and one of the main defendants, the KCSD, were actually on the same side. Even Judge Clark had to admit that they were in a "friendly adversarial" relationship. That was the natural result of his realigning the KCSD to become a defendant.

By the time of the trial, the defendants included the state of Missouri, the KCSD, several federal agencies, and a number of suburban school districts. Benson's case took four months to present. He called more than 140 witnesses and introduced 2,100 exhibits.

Even though technically a defendant, the school district basically seconded everything that Benson argued. But the federal agencies and suburban districts put up a stout defense, as did the state of Missouri.

In the end, the federal agencies were dismissed, as were the suburban school districts, by Judge Clark. The dismissal of the suburban districts was a major blow to Benson's case, for the relief he sought was a massive busing of students from the urban to suburban and suburban to urban schools. Judge Clark, however, was bound by Supreme Court precedent, which prevented him from ordering busing between school districts.

Clark's verdict was issued in September of 1984. It was an unusual opinion in that it rejected almost every argument and most of the evidence that Benson had offered. One by one, Judge Clark found contrary to Benson's claims against the remaining defendants—the state and the KCSD. He found no evidence that either had engaged in illegal discrimination. But, he still found that the KCSD was an unlawfully segregated school district because it was such in 1954, when *Brown v. Board of Education* was decided, and it was still segregated in 1984. The essence of his decision was that because of the state's pre-*Brown* racism, it was responsible for the segregated school district in 1984, even though the state had taken measures to comply with *Brown* between 1954 and 1984.

Judge Clark's decision was so unusual that many have tried to explain it. One justification was that Judge Clark was in a circuit (the Eighth) where the circuit court had been particularly aggressive in finding segregation everywhere. Being a new judge, this theory suggests that he had to find the KCSD to be unconstitutionally segregated, even where there was no evidence of it, lest the wrath of the circuit court descend upon him.

Another theory is that hearing four months' worth of witness after witness testifying of the harm of segregated schools left Judge Clark so affected that he had to find for the plaintiffs just so he could justify a remedy to end segregated schools.

The third suggestion, and one that Arthur Benson supported, was that Judge Clark harbored feelings of guilt for his rural upbringing, which likely included a degree of racism. He was bound and determined to make up for what he perceived to have been the injustice of the past.

Regardless of the judge's motivation, a finding had been made of unconstitutional segregation. The question that remained was what remedy would be ordered.

Because Judge Clark was perceived to possess a moderate judicial temperament, it was believed that he would do as most judges in the country faced with similar segregated school districts were doing: order some busing and the creation of a few magnet schools to encourage integration. Little did they know what was in Judge Clark's mind, as that mind was shaped by Arthur Benson in the following years.

JUDGE CLARK'S REMEDY

The Supreme Court had delivered great power into the hands of district court judges to fashion remedies for ending segregation in school districts. Little or no attention was paid to the qualifications such judges might or might not possess to make decisions affecting the education of schoolchildren.

Arthur Benson, who was to win almost all that he ever requested from Judge Russell Clark, was quite honest about Judge Clark's lack of qualifications for deciding what he did: "Here was a judge from a small town in south Missouri, who doesn't know anything about education except that his brother was a superintendent of schools. . . . How does a federal judge make sense of it?"[5]

Despite not having any credentials in education, Judge Clark was to demonstrate very little humility and no hesitance in approving plans proposed by others and adding to them in substantial ways.

Judge Clark ordered the state and the KCSD to submit separate plans for remedying the segregation that he had found existed. Arthur Benson, plaintiffs' attorney, worked with the defendant school district on their plan, and it was largely his product.

This is not the way the parties in most lawsuits work.

Relying on experts from the local university, Benson helped the district craft a plan that focused on educational improvements, in contrast to desegregation. The Benson-KCSD plan called for the reduction of class sizes, early childhood education programs, language development programs, the hiring of more counselors, a pre-college curriculum, and more. Benson had his expert witnesses testify before Judge Clark that creating these new programs and infusing the school system with new money would transform the district's heretofore failing teachers and principals into effective teachers and administrators. How? It just would. Benson's expert witnesses also testified that approval of the district's plan would result in the district's student achievement being raised to the national average within four or five years.

The proposed plan had a price tag of almost $69 million of new funding, a sum that was about three-quarters of the school district's current annual budget.

The state of Missouri offered a plan that was much more in line with what other federal judges were approving throughout the nation.

Ultimately, Judge Clark was to reject the state's proposed plan and to adopt the district's. In doing so, Judge Clark made it clear that cost was not an issue. He ordered the district to undertake almost everything that the plaintiffs had asked for, plus some. His ordered remedy cost almost $20 million more than the Benson-KCSD plan called for, and he required the state of Missouri to pay $67.5 million of the new funding and the district to come up with the remainder.

Further, he established a new entity, the Desegregation Monitoring Committee, to oversee the implementation of his ordered remedy. That twelve-member group was to become the most powerful force in the district—more powerful than the district's superintendent. It reported directly to Judge Clark, and whatever it ordered it got, for it operated with the direct authority of the federal court.

No one focused too much on the question of how the district, already struggling for funding, was to come up with its share of the cost of the remedial program. To assure that there were some funds available to the district, Judge Clark ordered what amounted to a tax increase. The state of Missouri had recently legislated a rollback of property taxes statewide. Judge Clark ordered that the tax rollback not take effect within the boundaries of the KCSD. Because the residents of the district did not receive the tax reduction, they suffered what amounted to a tax increase—by federal district court order. But, because property owners did not actually see their property taxes increase, this tax increase was hardly noticed, and it generated little publicity.

It was, however, a portend of what was coming.

The state was on the hook for the bulk of the new funding, and it did not like it. It appealed Judge Clark's decision to the Eight Circuit Court of Appeals, which upheld the judge's ruling. This was a pattern that was to be followed for the next many years: Benson asks, Judge Clark gives, circuit court upholds.

In his initial remedial order, Judge Clark ordered the district to investigate the best alternatives for magnet school programs. He wanted public surveys to explore what types of programs would appeal to students and their parents in not only the KCSD, specifically those parents who were sending their children to private schools, but the suburban school districts as well.

The survey results should have been very sobering to Arthur Benson and Judge Clark, for they showed little or no interest on the part of the parents of white students in either the suburban districts or the private schools within Kansas City. The percentage of white parents who were happy with their students' current schools ranged from 73 percent of suburban school parents to 90 percent of private school parents.

Despite this clear showing of the unlikelihood of success with magnet schools, Benson and his team went about designing an all-encompassing magnet school proposal. Judge Clark made it clear to them that they need not be concerned with what the proposal would cost.

Judge Clark stated his goal: All students enrolled in the KCSD should have educational opportunities equal to or better than those enjoyed by the students in the suburban districts.

When the state offered a program that called for far less in spending and, instead of massive new construction, an investment to eliminate health and safety hazards and to provide a good learning environment, Judge Clark rejected the plan. He called it a "patch and repair" that failed to meet the visual attractiveness he demanded. Only new school buildings would provide the appealing facilities the judge thought necessary.

The proposal eventually approved by Judge Clark was twofold. First, he approved the conversion of every high school and junior high school and one-half of the elementary schools into magnet schools. Benson and his experts predicted that this magnet school program would draw 11,000 students into the KCSD. It was projected that most of these would be white students from the suburbs or from local private schools, and thus the district would become integrated.

The magnet school conversion was projected to cost $143 million. Judge Clark ordered that the state pay $90 million of this amount and the school district the remainder. However, he also ordered that the state and school district were "jointly and severally liable" for whatever the bill was. This was the legalistic way of saying that if the KCSD did not have the money to pay its share, the state had to make up the difference.

It had become clear to the state of Missouri that Judge Clark was implementing a scheme that would constitute a raid on the state's treasury.

The state of Missouri had argued against much of what was ordered. Among the arguments it made was that the focus on the extraordinary and extravagant magnet school programs Judge Clark endorsed was undermining focus on what was most necessary—providing the students a basic, fundamental education. Its argument did not convince.

The second part of the plan approved by Judge Clark called for a massive infusion of capital to improve the buildings and facilities within the KCSD. He initially ordered over $250 million of capital improvements—this in a school district that had heretofore had an annual budget of $125 million.

The door was now opened wide.

HOW TO PAY? JUDGE CLARK, AKA KING GEORGE?

Before all of this money could be spent, there was the question of where it was going to come from. Even though Judge Clark had ordered the state to pay three-fourths of the cost of the remedial plan, the district had no way to raise the money to pay its one-fourth. Judge Clark was not daunted.

He had already ordered one tax increase on the citizens of the district; why not make it two—in fact, why not three?

Judge Clark first ordered a doubling of the property tax on residents of the district. Homeowners who owned a home appraised at $100,000 would see their property tax payment go from approximately $2,000 a year to $4,000 a year. He then added to that an entirely new tax on those who worked within the borders of the KCSD, whether they be residents or nonresidents of the district. That new tax was a surcharge on the Missouri state income tax, raising that income tax from 6 percent to 7.5 percent for those who were employed within the district. The judge justified this tax on nonresidents by stating that many of those who had fled the district still worked within it, and it was only fair that they be forced to pay for the segregation that their flight had created.

One man, two tax increases.

This time, this taxation without representation did not go unnoticed by the people of Kansas City and its suburbs. Protests were organized using ceremonial dropping of tea bags to connect the actions of Judge Russell Clark with King George of England. Public officials from the local county tax collector to the governor of the state spoke out against the judge's "tyranny."

The income tax surcharge, which was Judge Clark's own invention, created especially heated feedback and concern. Even Arthur Benson had to admit its impracticality. It raised so many questions about how it could be implemented that the state of Missouri was forced to hire twelve new employees to work on how to make it work. Ten new forms were created for tax filers to prepare.

It was, as some said, a perfect example of why state legislatures and not federal judges should impose taxes.

Judge Clark's tax increases, along with the remedial plan in general, were immediately contested, and an appeal was taken to the Eighth Circuit Court of Appeals. It approved Judge Clark's remedial plan with only slight modifications. It did reject the new income tax surcharge, but not because the circuit court had any concerns with its constitutionality.

On the issue of Judge Clark's raising the property tax, the Eight Circuit made a decision that is a classic "distinction without a difference." It said Judge Clark was fully empowered to raise property taxes himself. It did suggest, however, that in the future it might be better if Judge Clark simply authorized or ordered the district to raise taxes. If, as in Missouri, there were a state law that would have stood in the way of the district raising taxes beyond a certain amount, the district court could enjoin or prevent the state from enforcing the state law.

The case then went to the United States Supreme Court.

MISSOURI V. JENKINS

The state of Missouri asked the Supreme Court to rule not only on the constitutionality of a federal judge unilaterally raising taxes but on the appropriateness of Judge Clark's extraordinary remedial plan. The Court refused to address the plan. Thus, it was full speed ahead for the school district.

The issue before the Court that mattered was whether Judge Clark had it within his equitable powers to raise taxes unilaterally. The Eighth Circuit had done well in issuing an opinion that reflected a "distinction without a difference," and the Supreme Court proved its ability to do the same.

The Supreme Court ruled that Judge Clark had abused his discretion in ordering the property tax increase himself. But it held that Judge Clark did possess the power to order the district to raise taxes, and if the state had a law that stood in its way, the judge also had the equitable power to stop the state from enforcing the law.

The majority opinion was agreed to by five of the nine Justices. Four Justices dissented. In that dissent, the majority was exposed for suggesting that there was a difference between a judge issuing an order raising taxes and a judge ordering a school district to do so. Both were in violation of the Founders' intent to leave the raising of taxes to the legislative branch. Both were in direct conflict with the views of Hamilton that the judiciary did not have power over the purse.

The dissenters also argued that allowing judges to raise taxes was in direct violation of the due process of taxpayers—who had money extracted from them with no input. Those owners of real estate in Kansas City whose property tax was doubled by Judge Clark had no notice that such might happen and no opportunity to be heard before the tax was imposed.

The dissenters pointed to the fact that those who rebelled against the King of England did so, at least in part, because of their opposition to being taxed without being represented. Allowing unelected and unaccountable federal judges to raise taxes was no different. "Perhaps the KCMSD's Classical Greek theme schools emphasizing forensics and self-government will provide exemplary training in participatory democracy. But if today's dicta becomes law, such lessons will be of little use to students who grow up to become taxpayers in the KCMSD."[6]

They pointed out that one of the dangers of federal judges being empowered to raise taxes was that they could do so without themselves being subject to the increase—for if the judge did not live in the boundaries of the KCSD, the judge was not going to see his taxes doubled. Judge Clark lived in Springfield, Missouri, 175 miles away from Kansas City.

In sum, the dissenters argued that the power of taxation did not rest in the judicial branch or within those equitable powers that federal judges possessed. Their arguments, as passionately as they may have been expressed, did not convince one more Justice to switch opinions and to join with them.

Judge Clark's tax increase prevailed.[7]

THE KANSAS CITY SCHOOL DISTRICT "FIELD OF DREAMS"

Judge Clark was to end his involvement with the case in 1997. In the intervening years, he was to order dozens of additional expenditures. Eventually, the cost of the plan to end the segregation of the KCSD would total over $2 billion. The state of Missouri ended up paying over $1.5 billion of that amount.

What did this two billion dollars buy?

The district built fifteen new schools and rehabilitated over fifty more. Most of these schools were designed as "magnet schools" and offered programs in subjects such as computer and environmental science, foreign languages, and the ever-practical classical Greek athletics. At the foreign language immersion school, programs were offered in French, Spanish, and German. Teachers were recruited from Belgium, Cameroon, Puerto Rico, Argentina, and Germany. To make certain that the Greek athletic program was realistic, one school was provided a six-lane, indoor running track, weight rooms, racquetball courts, and an Olympic-quality gymnastics center.

One high school was designed to offer programs in heating and air conditioning, cosmetology, and robotics. Another was built with an Olympic-sized swimming pool that included an underwater viewing room.

A mock courtroom was constructed, and, to keep the experience authentic, it included a judge's chambers (office) and a jury deliberation room. A model United Nations was provided for, one that allowed for instantaneous language translation.

A twenty-five-acre wildlife sanctuary was created. This joined a two-thousand-square-foot planetarium, greenhouses, vivarium, arboretum, and zoo in providing unique educational opportunities for KCSD students. They also enjoyed professional quality recording, television, and animation studios. The television studio had rooms for editing and screening. A twenty-five-acre farm was also provided for the study of science. This farm had an air-conditioned meeting room that could handle meetings of more than 100 participants.

A large two-story library was built along with an art gallery for the use of the students.

A fencing team was formed that was to be coached by the fencing coach from the former Soviet Union. This team took field trips to Senegal and Mexico. One superintendent was sent on a goodwill mission to Moscow, Russia.

The teacher-to-student ratio in the district was an enviable 1 to 13. Parents in the district enjoyed the benefit of all-day kindergarten and, if the parents worked, there were before- and after-school programs.

The reason all this money was spent was to entice white students from the suburbs and from private schools within the KCSD. To facilitate their travel, an incredible bus system was improvised at a cost of $6.4 million. It featured door-to-door service. The number of bus routes increased from 100 to 850 under the magnet school plan. It was not unheard of to have one bus stop with ten students waiting to board ten different buses to take them to ten different schools.

On the chance that the 850 bus routes were not sufficient or convenient, private taxis would be sent to take the students from the suburbs to and from the school of their choice. Eventually, the district was paying $50,000 a month on taxis for students.

The magnet school program was too good not to be advertised to potential students, so a substantial program of television advertising and printed materials was undertaken. It was to cost almost $900,000 annually.

The KCSD was not known for its quality of administration prior to Judge Clark's showering it with largess. Its reputation was not enhanced in the years that followed.

Building and renovating schools in the numbers that were ordered, and with the urgency with which the judge demanded, created headaches for central administration. Adding to the construction demands were the immense number of purchases needed to implement the magnet school programs. It was just too much.

The district's annual budget rose from $125 million in 1985 to $432 million in 1992. This budget was double or triple that of a similar-sized school district anywhere else in the country.

Theft and embezzlement were rampant. The district was totally unprepared for the paperwork and oversight required for such an undertaking. "It was like taking a Third World country, a totally deprived community, and giving them unlimited wealth. And that's how they acted—like kids in a candy store. They misused it, mismanaged it, and misappropriated it. They were just not prepared for what Judge Clark thrust upon them."[8]

Examples of waste included purchasing computers that sat in a warehouse until they had become obsolete, buying $700 light fixtures, and obtaining new desks to replace practically new ones. Warehouses were full of supplies, furniture, and computers that never made it to the classroom.

To deal with the decision making and paperwork generated by the mass of construction and purchasing under way, the KCSD's central administration grew to be three to five times the size of similar-sized school districts. A 1991 audit showed that only 46 percent of the district's budget actually made it to the classroom; the rest was absorbed in administration and overhead.

Because Judge Clark's order required the state to pay not only its share but any deficit the district could not pay, the impact on the state of Missouri was substantial. The state complained that 44 percent of its entire public education budget was going to the 9 percent of students who attended school in Kansas City and St. Louis, a city that was also under a desegregation regimen.

Missouri was spending more to desegregate than it was spending on prisons, courts, the highway patrol, and the state fire marshal combined.

The parents of students in the state's other school districts could not ignore the fact that KCSD was awash in money while they were holding bake sales and car washes, abandoning field trips and extracurricular activities, and firing teachers because of their districts' declining funding.

But there was absolutely nothing they could do. The matter had been decided by the Supreme Court, and Judge Clark's Field of Dreams was being constructed.[9]

JUDGE CLARK'S GRAND SCHEME— WAS THE DREAM A SUCCESS?

In 1995, the parties were back before the Supreme Court. This time, the Court considered the merits of Judge Clark's remedial plan. It found that his focus on magnet schools to attract white students from the suburban school districts was not appropriate. Furthermore, the Court decided that Judge Clark's recent order increasing the salaries of all of the teachers

and the staff of the KCSD was beyond the judge's discretic

to focus only on the vestiges of prior discrimination and

trol of the school system back to local authorities as soon

essence, Judge Clark was now corralled. He could no lor

KCSD. Judge Clark ended his involvement in the case in

case officially ended in 2003.

What did Judge Clark's extravagant reconstruction

accomplish?

The short answer is, nothing.

If the proper measure of the dream was a more integr

trict, with the addition of 11,000 new white students as v

was a dismal failure. The largest number of white, suburb:

enrolled in one year was 1,500. Most of them did not r

ond year. By the 1996–97 school year, only 387 suburba

advantage of the door-to-door buses and taxis to attend

the KCSD. Given the fact that the district's annual deseg

was about $200 million, it was not a very good investmer

Judge Clark had been warned by the studies he had

parents of students in the suburbs and private schools w

their children's education. Those studies proved to be acc

With the construction of new schools, and oppositic

of old schools, the district ended up with classrooms for

but never exceeded 37,000 enrolled. Of those enrolled, t

and white students did not change in the way that the re

contemplated. The percentage of black students enroll

actually increased from the start of the desegregation

when it was 68.3 percent, to 68.8 percent in 1995. In

students made up 90 percent or more of the students at

schools, two middle schools, and ten elementary school:

If the proper measurement of the success of the exp

dent achievement testing, the results were even more

Judge Clark. The experts had testified, and Judge Clar

vinced, that the standard achievement scores of the d

would reach national averages within four to five years. Those scores did not change throughout the entire period. Further, the academic achievement gap between black and white students did not narrow.

One can imagine how discouraged Judge Clark must have been when a witness who appeared before him in 1997 testified, "But educationally, it hasn't changed any of the measurable outcomes."[10] That witness testified that scores on standardized tests had not risen at all. The average three-grade-level black-white achievement gap was as big as it always had been. Of perhaps most importance, the witness testified that having black students and white students attend the same schools had no positive effect on the educational attainment of the black student. In other words, integration had no effect on education.

The expenditure of $2 billion had not solved the travails of the KCSD. In October of 1999, the Missouri Board of Education found that the KCSD was a failure, and its accreditation was taken from it, the only school district in the state of Missouri to be so treated. The district was given two more years to improve its performance. Those troubles have continued. In 2010, it closed twenty-nine of its sixty-one schools. In 2011, it lost its accreditation again. Currently, it has a provisional accreditation.[11]

WHAT ARE THE CONSEQUENCES OF A
JUDICIARY WITHOUT LIMITS?

FEDERAL JUDGES' EQUITABLE POWERS—
TO TAX AND GOVERN

In the end, the case of *Missouri v. Jenkins* is not about whether spending large amounts of money to improve the education of students, black or white, is good or bad. It is not about whether court-ordered magnet schools to entice white students to transfer and integrate predominantly black schools is good or bad.

It is important to emphasize that all the major parties involved in *Missouri v. Jenkins* were motivated by the finest of intentions. No one

doubted that Arthur Benson sought the very best for his clients. Judge Clark sincerely believed that everything that he did would result in the end of a segregated school district and in increased academic achievement for disadvantaged students in the KCSD. Those who oversaw the program, although stretched beyond their capacities, did their best.

It is even more important to emphasize that the goals of desegregation and improved educational achievement were noble and worthwhile objectives. Those are not in question.

The true issue raised by the case of *Missouri v. Jenkins* is whether it is right for federal judges to possess the power to tax and to govern. It is the appropriateness of the power vested in federal judges, or judges of any stripe, to exercise their equitable powers in the way endorsed by the Supreme Court in this case.

In at least two cases subsequent to 1990, federal courts have ordered local governments to increase taxes, relying on *Missouri v. Jenkins.* Beyond the power to order tax increases, federal courts have relied on the equitable powers they have been sanctioned to exercise by the Supreme Court to manage state prisons, oversee the administration of mental hospitals, conduct environmental protection efforts, and direct public housing programs.[12]

In each of these instances, the federal judge has operated as a member of the judiciary that is exercising executive and legislative responsibilities. The judges have, in fact, governed.

Does the end justify the means? That is a question for each reader to decide.

NOTES

Epigraph: Federalist No. 48, February 1, 1788; in Spalding, ed., *Founders' Almanac*, 198.

1. See "History of the Federal Judiciary," accessed online at http://www.fjc.gov /history/home.nsf/page/judges_impeachments.html.

2. Hamilton, Jay, and Madison, *The Federalist,* 421.

3. For more information about the Court decisions and methods approved for

achieving integration in the decades after *Brown,* see Andrey, "Missing Half";
Dunn, *Complex Justice;* Parkman, *Missouri v. Jenkins.*

4. See Benson, *School Segregation;* Dunn, *Complex Justice.* Arthur Benson was the
attorney for the plaintiffs in the case of *Missouri v. Jenkins.*

5. Dunn, *Complex Justice,* 90.

6. *Missouri v. Jenkins,* 495 U.S. 33 (1990), 77.

7. See generally, *Missouri v. Jenkins,* 495 U.S. 33 (1990).

8. Ciotti, "Money," 8.

9. For details about the KCSD programs and costs, see Benson, *School Segregation;*
Ciotti, *Money;* Dunn, *Complex Justice; Missouri v Jenkins,* 495 U.S. 33 (1990).

10. Ciotti, *Money,* 19–20.

11. See Dunn, *Complex Justice,* 176; "Parents, Faculty Hopeful as KCPS System
Retains Provisional Accreditation," 1 Dec. 2015, accessed online at http://
www.kshb.com/news/education/we-are-on-the-right-path-kansas-city-public
-schools-system-retains-provisional-accreditation.

12. See *Bylinski v. City of Allen Park,* 8 F.Supp. 2d 965 (E. D. Mich. 1998); *Employers
Ins. of Wausau v. St. Clair Contractors, Inc.,* 2007 WL 1202378 (D. Idaho, 2007);
Missouri v. Jenkins, 515 U.S. 70, 126 (1995); Easton, "Dual Role," 1.

CHAPTER SEVEN

HOW THE SUPREME COURT PLAYED A CENTRAL ROLE IN REDEFINING THE VALUES AND CULTURE OF AMERICA

OBERGEFELL V. HODGES (2015)

"To allow the policy question of same-sex marriage to be considered and resolved by a select, patrician, highly unrepresentative panel of nine is to violate a principle even more fundamental than no taxation without representation: no social transformation without representation."

—*Justice Antonin Scalia*

A VERY DIFFERENT AMERICA

Let your imagination run wild and conjure up a nation much unlike the one we live in today.

In this America, television programs are wildly dissimilar to those that we watch today. No one swears. If a married couple is depicted in a bedroom, they are shown as sleeping in separate beds—which raises questions in the minds of children as to what is wrong with their parents. They will not get the answer to that question from watching television, for no depiction of overt sexual situations or sexuality is allowed. The portrayal of violence is subdued, and rarely do people actually bleed. The family depicted is almost always a man and a woman with a few children. The proper raising of children, including teaching them the importance of moral conduct, is a frequent program plotline.

The movies of this America are very different. Swearing is rare, used only to develop a character or to emphasize a storyline. It is not gratuitous. Sexuality is intimated, not graphically portrayed. Religions, or religious values, are commonly integral to the plot, and they are always depicted in a positive light. With very few exceptions, the good guys always win and right always prevails over wrong.

Popular music might be raucous, but it is never obscene. If it implies too much sexuality, it is banned from many if not most radio stations. Singers do not use coarse language, threaten violence, or mock that which is considered sacred by most Americans.

Drugs? Drugs are what you take to be healed.

In this imaginary country, teenagers still get in trouble sometimes. Occasionally, unmarried girls get pregnant, but it is expected that the father of the child will marry the girl. If not, the child is born and raised by the girl's family or given up for adoption. The peers of the couple do not celebrate the out-of-wedlock immorality—it is frowned upon, and the couple is sometimes scorned. An abortion is not considered an option.

To discourage sexual relations outside the bonds of marriage, laws exist that make fornication and adultery illegal. Birth control and contraceptives are difficult to obtain, particularly for the single person.

In this alternate world, marriage is considered essential to a happy life. Children are a priority. The raising of children by a mother and a father is normal. Almost all children are being raised in a home with a mother and a father.

Obscene magazines and movies are against the law. Those who produce them can be subject to federal and state prosecutions. Magazines that are pornographic and salacious, but not deemed legally obscene, come through the mail and are wrapped in plain brown paper so as to hide them from neighbors.

In this alternate America, there is evil and there are wicked men and women, but they strive assiduously to hide their wicked ways. They are not accepted or approved by the rest of society. They do not flaunt their rejection of accepted morality.

What a weird and different place!

To anyone older than half a century, this alternate world is not beyond their ability to perceive. No, this is the world they grew up in. It was the United States of America fifty years ago.

What changed? Who was responsible for the change?

There was a time, less than a lifetime ago, when federal law prohibited the use of the U.S. postal system for mailing materials that were deemed to be obscene, and state and local governments could prevent materials that were deemed to be obscene from being distributed in their territory.

Into the last half of the twentieth century, states could prohibit the showing of movies that were deemed to be obscene or immoral.

Within the last twenty years, there were states in which it was unlawful for unmarried people to engage in sexual relations.

There was a time, less than a few decades gone by, when both the federal and state governments regulated access to contraceptive and birth control supplies. States also outlawed abortions and sodomy.

There was a time, not very long ago, when elected state legislatures had the ability to define marriage.

That America was a very different country from the one in which we live today.

Again the question, what changed? Who changed it? What led to this dramatic transformation in the culture and society of America? How did the United States of America become such a different nation in a few short decades?

The quickest given and most widely accepted answer is that Hollywood and the media changed—and America changed with them.

However, the role that the United States Supreme Court has played in this transformation cannot be overlooked. Many of these efforts to redefine the values and culture of America have been aided, at least in part, by decisions of the United States Supreme Court. In fact, a case could be made that the Supreme Court has been the primary agent of social transformation in our country.

If that is provable, the question that it raises is whether, in a republic like ours, such is the proper role for the Court. Should our nation have been fundamentally transformed by decisions of the nine lawyers of the Supreme Court?

ANTHONY COMSTOCK: THE CONSCIENCE OF NINETEENTH-CENTURY AMERICA

At the end of the American Civil War, some Americans feared that their nation was undergoing a moral deterioration. As is always the case in war, immorality had shadowed the troops. Many of America's soldiers came home from war having formed habits that were considered to be evil and unacceptable in ordinary times. New immigrants were flooding America in the last decades of the 1800s, and some saw in them unacceptable permissiveness when it came to matters of sex. Women were experiencing opportunities outside of the home, and many deemed that to be a threat to the family.

Anthony Comstock was a farm boy from rural Connecticut who was appalled at what he witnessed in New York City when he moved there after serving in the Civil War. He was a devout Christian, and he perceived in the wickedness he observed on the streets of New York—specifically prostitutes and pornography—that something was wrong with America.

He decided to lead a moral renewal in America.

He became the head of the New York Society for the Suppression of Vice. It was a well-funded organization, finding favor with many of the city's wealthiest citizens. In 1873, his personal lobbying resulted in the passage by Congress of what became known as the Comstock Law of 1873. It made it a federal crime, subject to a fine or imprisonment at hard labor, for possessing, selling, lending, giving away, exhibiting, publishing, or using the United States mail to send any obscene materials, or drugs, medicines, or instructive materials for the prevention of conception or for causing abortions.

Comstock's motivation for pushing for the legislation, and then enforcing it with much gusto, was complicated. A close friend had died of venereal disease, and Comstock blamed pornography for his friend's descent into depravity. He also feared the harmful impact of pornography on children. Comstock and those who supported him believed that contraception promoted promiscuity and immoral behavior. Abortion was targeted because the primitive procedures used in abortions often resulted in serious physical harm to women. It was also believed that abortions encouraged immoral behavior.

Comstock got himself appointed as a special agent of the postal service. He functioned as such for the next forty-two years. Later in life he bragged that he had successfully prosecuted more than 3,600 violators of his law and had been responsible for destroying 160 tons of materials that defied the law.

During the same period, roughly 1880 through the start of the First

World War, there was a movement called the Social Purity Movement, which focused on the elimination of prostitution and pornography and the raising of the age of consent for premarital sex to protect the innocence of young women.

Half of the states followed the lead of Comstock and passed laws to outlaw obscene materials. Thirty states had laws limiting the distribution of contraceptive materials. Most states put limits on abortions. Many if not most states had laws to criminalize fornication, adultery, and sodomy. Criminal prosecutions for fornication and adultery became more common, peaking between 1890 and 1910.

The Comstock Act was the leading indicator of America's cultural and moral priorities for almost 100 years, and its proscriptions became the target of cases that eventually made their way to the United States Supreme Court.[1] What follows is a recital of some of the ways that our nation was transformed as the Supreme Court decided those cases.

PORNOGRAPHY AND OBSCENITY— PROTECTED BY THE CONSTITUTION?

The First Amendment to the Constitution of the United States protects speech and press from infringement by the government. These are among the most basic of our rights and have been doggedly protected by the courts. But there are two areas of speech or print that the Supreme Court has said do not deserve protection, and those are pornographic materials that are obscene and child pornography.

The first of these exceptions invites the question—what is obscene? The Supreme Court did not have to decide that question for the first 150-plus years of our nation's life. That fact alone is stark evidence of the relative innocence of that long-ago period in our history.

It was not until 1957 that the Supreme Court was forced to squarely decide a case involving obscenity. In that decision, the Court stated without equivocation that obscenity was not protected under the First Amendment. The Court then attempted to define what obscenity was, but did so with a standard that was notably vague and imprecise.

Thereafter, the Supreme Court found itself inundated with cases in which defendants found guilty of violating either federal or state anti-obscenity acts appealed their convictions to the Court. The Court struggled mightily to define obscenity in a way that would give fair warning to people that they might be violating laws prohibiting it.

It proved to be very difficult. The Justices attempted to deal with these appeals on a case-by-case basis. That was disturbing from a purely legal standpoint, for how were individuals to know whether they were dealing with illegally obscene material before the Supreme Court considered their specific cases? It was also difficult for the Justices on a personal level, as they were forced to read or view printed materials or movies that had been the basis for the lower court convictions. This did not sit well with many of the Justices.

In one case, a Justice admitted that prohibited obscenity was very hard to define, but that he knew it when he saw it. That standard did not give much help to either prosecutors or defendants.

A number of Justices objected to any regulation of obscenity. They did not believe it fell within the power of government to limit what adults could read or view within their own homes. They were willing to acknowledge that government could legitimately attempt to prevent children from gaining access to obscene materials, but they also argued that those efforts could not be used to limit the access of adults to whatever they wanted to consume.

The notion that an adult should be free to consume whatever he or she wanted became the theory upon which obscenity cases were eventually decided. As a practical matter, states lost their ability to prevent an adult from consuming obscene materials. The Court limited the states' use of the police power to control obscenity to its production and transmission.

Over time, the states lost their ability to control even those.

In 1973, the Court came up with a definition of illegal obscenity that it thought would provide a firm and permanent definition. In the case of *Miller v. California,* it ruled that a state could outlaw materials that the average person, applying current community standards, found to appeal to prurient interest and that did not contain literary, artistic, political, or scientific value.[2]

That standard remains the legal definition of obscenity today. Its primary value is that it permits consideration of the differences that exist from community to community throughout our nation; what might be acceptable in New York City might not be acceptable in a small town in the rural Midwest.

What was considered the definition's strength has become its greatest weakness, however.

With the emergence of national and even international sources of pornography—cable television and the Internet—the ability of state governments to regulate the transmission of obscene materials has become all but impossible. As a practical matter, any adult can access anything he or she wants to read or view. Very little effort is undertaken to regulate pornography—even that which under the *Miller* test would be considered obscene and therefore not protected by the First Amendment.

To the extent any level of government is still trying, it is Congress. Its efforts have focused almost exclusively on trying to keep obscene materials away from children. Those efforts have largely failed.

Congress has tried. In 1996 it passed a law requiring cable television providers to block sexually oriented programming during hours when children might be watching television. Regulations issued pursuant to the law required that such programming be confined to broadcast during the hours of ten in the evening to six in the morning. The Supreme Court ruled that the statute was unconstitutional.[3]

The Internet has become the chief means by which pornography and obscenity enter the homes of Americans. As the Internet grew in popularity, its growth was largely fueled by those seeking pornography, much of it illegally obscene. Congress reacted by passing the Communications Decency Act of 1996, which criminalized the Internet transmission of "obscene or indecent" materials, or materials "patently offensive as measured by contemporary community standards," to those under the age of eighteen. The Supreme Court found the statute to be in violation of the First Amendment the next year.[4]

In response, Congress passed the Child Online Protection Act in 1998. By this legislation, the Congress again attempted to prohibit the Internet transmission of materials that were harmful to minors. In defining what such materials were, Congress referred to the "contemporary community standards" test that the Supreme Court had endorsed in 1973 and had never departed from. This legislation was immediately challenged for relying on that standard in light of the worldwide reach of the Internet.

The case made its way to the Supreme Court in 2002. The Court refused to find the act unconstitutional on the basis of its reliance on the community standard, but a number of Justices expressed concern with the legislation's reliance on that standard. For example, Justice Stephen Breyer stated that when Congress made reference to "community standards," it must have been referring to the country's adult community taken as a whole. He argued that for the Court to find that it referred to a local community would allow "the most puritan of communities" to have a veto over the nation's Internet.[5]

What would such a national "adult community" standard be? In 1983, a judge on the Second Circuit Court of Appeals suggested that the community standards of New York are so low that nothing would be deemed to be obscene.[6]

The case was sent back to lower courts. Two years later, the case came before the Supreme Court again, not for a final determination on the merits, but on the issue of whether an injunction should be issued preventing the United States from enforcing the law. The Supreme Court held that it was likely that the 1998 act was unconstitutional.

The lower courts continued to hear arguments on the act's possible violation of the First Amendment. In 2008, the Third Circuit Court declared the act unconstitutional on a number of grounds, including the fact that it had relied on the community standard.

An appeal was filed with the Supreme Court, but it refused to hear the case.[7] Thus, the 1998 act is void. Ironically, it is void in part because of its reliance on the Supreme Court's own "community standard" test for obscenity.

Child pornography has been deemed by the Supreme Court to deserve no protection under the First Amendment. But even in this area, the Court has weakened efforts to protect innocent children from exposure to this most horrible form of pornography.

In 1996, Congress passed a law prohibiting "virtual child pornography," images of a minor engaging in sexual conduct in which the minor is the creation of a computer or an adult who looks like a minor is used. Experience has shown that people who want to entice minors into sexual activity often use child pornography to break down the minors' defenses. This was one of the reasons for passage of the 1996 act: to limit, if even in a small way, the amount of child pornography that would be available for that purpose.

The Supreme Court declared the act unconstitutional in 2002.[8]

Technically, obscenity, as defined by the Supreme Court in the *Miller* case of 1973, is still not protected by the Constitution. However, Supreme Court decisions have made it nearly impossible for obscenity to be banned. Federal obscenity laws are rarely enforced. States have been thwarted in almost every effort to keep obscene materials from their citizens. Because of that, our nation is awash with pornography, much of it legally obscene. Its impact on the minds and lives of the American people is the subject of considerable academic study and discussion among social scientists, psychologists, and ethicists.

THE SUPREME COURT AND THE MOVIES

Arguably, the saga of the American movie industry has gone full circle—salacious (relatively speaking), to moral and proper, and back to salacious. The Supreme Court played a significant role in the last two stages of that cycle.

The cinema emerged as a major contributor to American culture in the early decades of the twentieth century. In its infancy, the industry suffered a number of high-profile scandals involving movie stars that upset the decidedly moral populace of that era. Hollywood also inflicted injury to itself by producing a handful of movies that were deemed indecent for the broad public. In reaction, states began to censor films that did not meet the standards deemed appropriate for their citizenry.

In 1915, the Supreme Court determined that the states had the authority to do so. In a unanimous decision considering an Ohio statute that created a board of censors for motion picture films, the Court ruled that states could censor or prohibit movies that were not deemed to be moral. The Court ruled that movies were not entitled to free speech protection.[9]

Thereafter, other states quickly entered the arena. By 1921, thirty-seven states either had or were considering legislation that would allow them to determine which films could be shown within their states.

Hollywood realized that it had a serious problem. In reaction, it created a Motion Picture Production Code—a set of moral guidelines that movies were expected to abide by. The Code prohibited profanity, depiction of licentiousness or nudity, ridicule of the clergy, or willful offense to any nation, race, or creed. It required that special caution be exercised in depicting certain scenes or themes, for example, the use of drugs, sympathy for criminals, and men and women sharing the same bed.

The Code ruled the industry for several decades. Many within the industry bridled at the restraints they were forced to operate under, but the Code remained in place. It was enforced with some strictness because the movie studios realized that the states were in a position to respond with censorship should the industry stray too far from what the Code required.

In 1952, however, that threat was considerably weakened. In a case involving the censoring board in the state of New York, the Supreme Court decided that a movie could not be withheld from the public because it was deemed to be sacrilegious. In question was a New York statute that required the prior approval and licensing of movies. If a movie was deemed to be obscene, indecent, immoral, or sacrilegious, it could be banned. The Supreme Court reversed its decision from 1915 and held that movies were entitled to First Amendment protection. The Court carefully crafted its ruling to apply only to movies banned for being sacrilegious, saying that it was not preventing a state from banning a movie for being obscene.[10]

But the fact that the Supreme Court attached First Amendment status to movies led to an inevitable result.

Seeing the possibilities, the movie industry moved quickly. The Code was pushed against and violated by prominent directors and producers. The competition of television and foreign-produced films motivated the movie industry to look for ways to keep its prominent position as the first choice for the entertainment dollar.

By the 1960s, the Code was all but history. In 1968, it was replaced by the current rating system for movies.

The Supreme Court aided the movie industry in removing the shackles of state censorship. Its 1973 *Miller* decision, defining what was obscene, opened the door for it to rule against a Georgia statute outlawing the showing of obscene movies in Georgia. At question was the 1974 conviction of a Georgia theater owner who had shown the movie *Carnal Knowledge*. A jury found the movie to be obscene under the Georgia statute, which defined obscenity more strictly than did the Supreme Court in *Miller*. The Justices determined (after viewing the film) that it was not obscene under its 1973 definition.[11] State censorship laws became irrelevant.

To judge the impact of the Supreme Court's attaching First Amendment protection to movies, one need only spend time watching movies from the 1930s to the 1950s and contrasting them with movies produced today.[12]

GRISWOLD—HOW A CASE ABOUT CONTRACEPTION GAVE BIRTH TO THE RIGHT OF PRIVACY

Thus far in this chapter, the discussion has focused on the Supreme Court's transformative powers under the First Amendment. The Supreme

Court's discovery of the "right to privacy" vested in the Court an entirely separate arsenal for reshaping America.

Following passage of the Federal Comstock Act in 1873, many states passed their own laws to regulate the distribution of contraceptive materials and to limit access to abortions. As late as the 1960s, many states still had laws prohibiting or restricting the sale and use of contraceptives.

None of the states equaled the state of Connecticut in regulating the use of contraceptives. Connecticut made the use of any drug or device for the purpose of preventing conception illegal. It also made it a crime to assist someone else to prevent pregnancy. The law applied to married couples as well as singles. It was rarely enforced.

In 1965, the Supreme Court was asked to decide whether the Connecticut law was constitutional. It is likely that this case challenging contraceptive laws purposely arose out of Connecticut because its law was so extreme.

The state argued that its law was justified in order to discourage infidelity of married individuals. The Supreme Court was not convinced.

In the majority opinion, the Justices found that although it was nowhere specifically found in the words of the Constitution, there were attached to several of the rights included in the Bill of Rights certain "penumbras." Those penumbras were formed by "emanations" that gave those rights life and substance. Among those penumbras was a right to privacy against government intrusion.

The Justices who held this opinion focused extensively on the right of privacy of the married couple. "Would we allow the police to search the sacred precincts of marital bedrooms for telltale signs of the use of contraceptives? The very idea is repulsive. . . . We deal with a right of privacy older than the Bill of Rights. . . . Marriage is . . . intimate to the degree of being sacred."[13]

And thus was born the "right of privacy." It was conceived rather late in our nation's history, but its belatedness has not stunted its influence— as will be seen.

The justification for overturning Connecticut's law, the sacredness of marriage, was cast aside just seven years later. In a case involving a Massachusetts law that prohibited the dispensing of contraceptives to unmarried persons, the Court again struck the legislation.

The law had been passed in 1879. In a 1917 opinion, the Massachusetts Supreme Court had declared that among the purposes of the statute were the desire to protect purity and chastity, to encourage self-restraint, and to defend the sanctity of the home. In its argument before the Supreme Court of the United States some fifty years later, the state added the further justification of protecting public health. The Court declared that such justifications were not served by the prohibition. It announced that the right of privacy extended to both married and single adults and that it included the right to decide to bear a child without government interference.[14]

Five years later, the Supreme Court rejected the effort of the state of New York to keep contraceptives from those under the age of sixteen, asserting that the Constitutional right of privacy extends the right to decide whether to become pregnant to minors as well as adults.[15]

In the end, the Supreme Court has elevated the right to privacy, which includes the individual's right to determine when one becomes pregnant, above the state's interest in discouraging out-of-wedlock births, infidelity, or immorality among its citizens.

STATE LAWS PROHIBITING FORNICATION AND ADULTERY

In a concurring opinion in *Griswold,* several Justices stated that one of the reasons they found the Connecticut ban on contraception unconstitutional was because the state had other means of discouraging infidelity—referring specifically to Connecticut laws that prohibited adultery and fornication. These Justices argued that the constitutionality of such laws was clear.

It was not quite so clear a few years later.

As of 2014, eighteen states had laws that made it a crime to commit adultery or fornication. These statutes are rarely enforced, and have not been for several decades. Still, efforts to remove them from the criminal codes are usually opposed and often fail.[16]

The question is not whether the statutes are enforced, but whether they are, as the concurring Justices in *Griswold* said, clearly constitutional.

As late as 1986, the answer was "yes." In that year, the Supreme Court considered a case that arose out of the state of Georgia. That state had a law making it a crime to engage in acts of sodomy. The law was challenged for its constitutionality, the argument being that the recently identified, constitutionally protected right of privacy included the right for adults to engage in acts of sodomy.

The majority of members of the Supreme Court held that there was no fundamental right thus protected. In response to the argument that the only basis for the law was the belief by a majority of Georgians that sodomy was immoral and unacceptable, the majority wrote: "This is said to be an inadequate rationale to support the law. The law, however, is constantly based on notions of morality, and if all laws representing essentially moral choices are to be invalidated under the Due Process Clause, the courts will be very busy indeed."[17]

Chief Justice Warren Burger joined in the majority opinion, but he added the point that sodomy had been proscribed since ancient times and therefore it would be impossible to find it to be a fundamental right. To do so would be to "cast aside millennia of moral teaching."[18]

These two references to morality as the justification for state laws triggered a stern response from one of the Justices who dissented from the Court's majority opinion. Justice Stevens argued, "[The] fact that the governing majority in a State has traditionally viewed a particular practice as immoral is not a sufficient reason for upholding a law prohibiting the practice."[19]

Based on the *Bowers* decision, state laws that prohibited fornication and adultery then on the books were, in fact, constitutional.

In 1986, Justice Stevens lost the argument that laws based upon a majority of citizens' views of morality were invalid. He might have lost the battle, but just seventeen years later, he won the war.

In the 2003 case of *Lawrence v. Texas,* the Supreme Court reversed its decision of 1986 in *Bowers.* It ruled as unconstitutional a Texas law that criminalized sodomy. Of greatest importance, it held that Justice Stevens's view was correct that the governing view of morality cannot be the basis for laws prohibiting a practice.

The majority opinion relied on the concept of substantive due process that was given birth by the case of *Lochner v. New York* (discussed in chapter 3) to justify its decision. The majority chose to provide its own definition of what liberty includes:

> These matters, involving the most intimate and personal choices a person may make in a lifetime, choices central to personal dignity and autonomy, are central to the liberty protected by the Fourteenth Amendment. At the heart of liberty is the right to define one's own concept of existence, of meaning, of the universe, and of the mystery of human life.[20]

The reference to "personal dignity" as a protected liberty interest was new to the case law. Its importance was to grow exponentially, just as had the right of privacy.

Justice Scalia wrote a forceful dissent. He was prescient in much of what he said. Most directly, he noted the sea change that the majority had endorsed—that it was now a constitutional principle that a moral view held by the majority of citizens could never be an acceptable justification for laws. He predicted that this would lead, inevitably, to the striking of all laws against fornication, bigamy, adultery, and obscenity. He also contended that it was inevitable that the traditional view of marriage would be struck down.

One year later, relying on *Lawrence* in part, the Massachusetts Supreme Judicial Court held that same-sex couples could not be barred from marriage.[21]

Two years later, the supreme court of the state of Virginia declared its antifornication laws unconstitutional, based upon *Lawrence.*[22]

OBERGEFELL V. HODGES—JUSTICE SCALIA'S PROPHECY IS FULFILLED

Thirteen years after *Lawrence,* a case made its way to the Supreme Court in which Justice Scalia's speculation about the future of traditional marriage was to be tested. The result of the case was a transformation of marriage in America.

It was not the first time that the question of same-sex marriage had come before the Supreme Court. In 1972, two men sought a marriage license in the state of Minnesota. When it was denied, the couple challenged the Minnesota law, which allowed marriage only between a man and a woman. The supreme court of Minnesota upheld the constitutionality of the Minnesota law. The case, *Baker v. Nelson,* was appealed to the United States Supreme Court. The Court issued a terse, eleven-word decision, "The appeal is dismissed for want of a substantial federal question." This opinion, short to the extreme, was still a decision on the merits by the Court, and the case constituted a precedent. The Court was saying that there was no constitutional right to same-sex marriage.[23]

It was not long thereafter that a popular movement to allow same-sex marriages was launched.

Much of the social transformation wrought by popular culture, Hollywood, and the media, as aided, abetted, and protected by court action, has been begrudgingly accepted by the American people. Many Americans may not like the way that our culture has been transformed, but when such changes have been endorsed by the Supreme Court, they have largely acquiesced.

That is not true for all cases. The Court's discovery of the right of privacy to abortion is the most notable example. *Roe v. Wade* remains not only controversial but actively opposed more than forty years after it was decided.

Protection of traditional marriage may be similar to opposition to unlimited abortion. As society began to perceive the impending challenge to traditional marriage, efforts were undertaken to go on the offense. One of the first responses came from Congress. In 1996, it passed the Defense of Marriage Act, which defined marriage under federal laws, including the IRS Code, as excluding same-sex partners.

The most significant effort undertaken to protect traditional marriage was the introduction of an amendment to the Constitution of the United States, the Federal Marriage Amendment. It defined marriage in the United States as the union of a man and a woman. The proposed amendment was introduced in 2002 and again in each Congress for the next three Congressional sessions. Votes were taken, and, although a majority of the members of Congress supported the amendment, it never did receive the support of the two-thirds of the members of both the House and the Senate required to send the amendment to the states for ratification.

Meanwhile, those who wanted to alter the institution of marriage moved forward. By 2013, a number of states permitted same-sex couples to marry, either through court decree, state legislative action, or popular vote. One of those was the state of New York. A case arose from that state in which one partner of a same-sex marriage had passed away and the survivor wanted to claim the federal estate tax exemption for surviving spouses. It was denied by the IRS because of the Defense of Marriage Act. The surviving spouse sued the United States, challenging the validity of the act.

The case, *United States v. Windsor,* made its way to the Supreme Court. In a 2013 decision, in which five members of the Court agreed and four disagreed, the Court struck the Defense of Marriage Act as unconstitutional. One of the primary reasons given by the majority was a states' rights justification. The opinion noted that historically states had the right to decide questions of marriage. The state of New York had granted the right for same-sex couples to marry, but the federal government was interfering with that right by denying certain benefits that were under federal jurisdiction.

The majority opinion also continued the theme that the right of same-sex couples to marry was a ratification of the couple's "personal dignity." Reference to the importance of "dignity" was sprinkled throughout the opinion.[24]

The *Windsor* case was a herald of what was to come. Following this case, a number of lower courts ruled that state laws or constitutions that defined marriage as the union of a man and a woman were unconstitutional. The Supreme Court took the case of *Obergefell v. Hodges* involving four states that defined marriage in the traditional way. It issued its decision in June of 2015.

Because the *Windsor* decision emphasized the importance of states' rights, some believed that the most likely outcome of *Obergefell* would be a decision that allowed each state to decide the definition of marriage. Those who hoped so were to be disappointed. The importance of states' rights had lost its potency in the two years after *Windsor.*

In *Obergefell,* the 1972 case of *Baker v. Nelson* was specifically overturned. In an opinion that represented the viewpoint of five members of the Court, the Supreme Court ordered that same-sex couples be allowed to marry in all states that prohibited it. All state laws and constitutional provisions to the contrary were voided.

The justification for its ruling was plainly and simply substantive due process as given birth by the case of *Lochner v. New York* in 1905—the power exercised by any five members of the Court to define or to redefine what the word *liberty* means. "The identification and protection of fundamental rights is an enduring part of the judicial duty to interpret the Constitution."[25]

Relying upon concepts such as the need for "individual autonomy," "self-definition," and "dignity," and characterizing it as "a liberty that remains urgent in our own era," the majority held that the right for same-sex couples to marry was a fundamental right inherent in "the liberty of the person."

The four members of the Court who dissented did so with particular vigor. Chief Justice Roberts pointed out that for a right to be fundamental, it had to have been accepted in the past. Same-sex marriage did not fit that category. He noted that the traditional meaning of marriage, which had been accepted in every culture since the beginning of human history, was hardly an irrational position for states to hold on to. He also chided the majority for attaching constitutional protection to concepts as vague as "dignity."

The minority discussed the similarities of the *Obergefell* opinion with the once scorned decision of *Lochner v. New York*. In their minds, a return to the Supreme Court positioning itself as had the *Lochner* Court was fraught with risk.

Among their most barbed criticism, the dissenters pointed out that the majority opinion dangerously offended our system of self-government. They argued that it terminated the democratic debate that the nation had been engaged in for a relatively short period of time—that the decision reflected not what the law *was* but what five people *thought* it should be.

They suggested that eliminating the democratic process came with risks, especially to those who would continue to oppose same-sex marriage on religious grounds. Justice Roberts noted that it might lead to the loss of tax-exempt status for those religious organizations that continued to support traditional marriage.

As usual, the dissent that was the most forceful came from Justice Scalia:

> The substance of today's decree is not of immense personal importance to me. The law can recognize as marriage whatever sexual attachments and living arrangements it wishes. . . . So it is not of special importance to me what the law says about marriage. It is of overwhelming importance, however, who it is that rules me. Today's decree says that my Ruler, and the Ruler of 320 million Americans coast-to-coast, is a majority of the nine lawyers on the Supreme Court. . . . This practice of constitutional revision by an unelected committee of nine, always accompanied (as it is today) by extravagant praise of liberty, robs the People of the most important liberty they asserted in the Declaration of Independence and won in the Revolution of 1776: the freedom to govern themselves.[26]

WHERE IS AMERICA HEADED ON OTHER KEY QUESTIONS AFFECTING THE CHARACTER OF OUR NATION?

WHAT NEXT?

The answers to certain questions lie ahead of us—and those questions suggest that interesting times may be anticipated.

For example, in the Supreme Court's majority opinion in *Obergefell,* the contention that liberty under our Constitution included the individual's right to "dignity" was made nine times. Where are our elected officials to find guidance as to what is, or is not, an infringement of a person's right to dignity?

The sum and substance of the social transformation either initiated or endorsed by the Supreme Court of the United States is what is often referred to as the "sexual revolution." The end result of this upheaval is sexual relations without consequences. Where does this lead our society and culture in the long run? Does it, in fact, make us a better society? Is our culture enriched or debased? Does it result in a happier society?

Will *Obergefell* be accepted and forgotten, or will it continue to be a source of contention into the future? In a remarkable rebuke of the Supreme Court, more than sixty scholars and informed citizens called upon elected officials to refuse to accept that decision as binding precedent.[27] It is clear that those who continue to support traditional marriage, especially if their support is based on religious conviction, remain on a collision course in many arenas with those who support same-sex marriage.

To those who treasure our right to govern ourselves, the most important question we face is where does the soft tyranny of the Supreme Court end? One can agree, in whole or in part, with the way that our nation has been transformed by Supreme Court decisions. For example, one can argue that in protecting obscenity, the First Amendment to the Constitution was being protected. One can find justifications and defensible arguments for the removal of state prohibitions on the distribution of contraceptives, in favor of same-sex marriage, and so on. But, again, with what issue will the Supreme Court's transformative powers cease?

Whether one agrees or disagrees with the social transformation in our society and culture over the last half century, it is of no small importance to answer the question: Does the end justify the means? Are we, in fact, better off as a free people to have so much change in our way of life dictated by five members of the Supreme Court—none of whom ever have to make an accounting of their decisions?

NOTES

Epigraph: *Obergefell v. Hodges,* 135 S.Ct. 2584, 2629 (2015).

1. For information on the Comstock Act, see <a ref="http://law.jrank.org /pages/5508/Comstock-Law-1873.html">Comstock Law of (1873)</a>; http://www.pbs.org/wgbh/amex/pill/peopleevents/e_comstock.html; https:// www.britannica.com/event/Comstock-Act; see also Sweeny, "Undead Statutes."
2. *Miller v. California,* 413 U.S. 15 (1973); see also Woodward and Armstrong, *The Brethren,* 231–246, 294–306, 336–339, 441–443, 488–489 for accounts of the Justices' struggles to define obscenity.
3. *United States v. Playboy Entertainment Group,* 529 U.S. 803 (2000).
4. *Reno v. American Civil Liberties Union,* 521 U.S. 844 (1997).
5. *Ashcroft v. American Civil Liberties Union,* 535 U.S. 564, 590 (2002).
6. *U.S. v. Various Articles of Obscene Merchandise,* 709 F.2d 132, 138 (2d. Cir.1983).
7. See *American Civil Liberties Union v. Mukasey,* 534 F.3d 181 (3d Cir. 2008) and 555 U.S.1137 (2009).
8. *Ashcroft v. The Free Speech Coalition,* 535 U.S. 234 (2002).
9. *Mutual Film Corporation v. Industrial Commission of Ohio,* 35 S.Ct. 387 (1915).
10. *Joseph Burstyn Inc. v. Wilson,* 343 U.S. 495 (1952).
11. *Jenkins v. Georgia,* 94 S.Ct. 2750 (1974). See also Woodward and Armstrong, *The Brethren,* 337–338.
12. For information about the Motion Picture Production Code, see https:// en.wikipedia.org/wiki/Motion_Picture_Production_Code.
13. *Griswold v. State of Connecticut,* 85 S.Ct. 1678, 1682 (1965).
14. *Eisenstadt v. Baird,* 92 S.Ct.1029 (1972).
15. *Carey v. Population Services International,* 97 S.Ct. 2010 (1977).

16. Sweeny, "Undead Statutes."

17. *Bowers v. Hardwick,* 106 S.Ct. 2841, 2846 (1986).

18. Ibid., 2847.

19. Ibid., 2857.

20. *Lawrence v. Texas,* 539 U.S. 558, 574 (2003).

21. *Goodridge v. Department of Public Health,* 798 N.E.2d 941 (2003).

22. *Martin v. Ziherl,* 607 S.E.2d 367 (2005).

23. *Baker v. Nelson,* 93 S.Ct. 37 (1972).

24. *United States v. Windsor,* 133 S.Ct. 2675 (2013).

25. *Obergefell v. Hodges,* 135 S.Ct. 2584, 2598 (2015).

26. Ibid., 2626–2627.

27. Statement is found at https://americanprinciplesproject.org/founding
-principles/statement-calling-for-constitutional-resistance-to-obergefell-v
-hodges%E2%80%AF/.

CONCLUSION

"The germ of dissolution of our federal government is
in the constitution of the federal Judiciary working like
gravity by night and by day, gaining a little today and a
little tomorrow, and advancing its noiseless step like a thief,
over the field of jurisdiction, until all shall be usurped."

—*Thomas Jefferson*

THE SUPREME COURT'S AMERICA

A sketch of America, as transformed and shaped by decisions of the Supreme Court, is as follows:

We live in a nation where five members of the Supreme Court, by virtue of the power of judicial review, have the final say in all matters of Constitutional interpretation. More tellingly, because the majority of major policy disputes and political issues somehow become decisions for the judicial branch to make, the Supreme Court has the final say in almost all decisions that matter in our country. The power vested in the federal courts includes the power to raise taxes, even for the most misguided yet noble effort.

Sadly, we remain a nation where race is the primary lens through which much human interaction is viewed. Relationships between the races are strained. Had the Supreme Court not sanctioned more than a half a century of state-sponsored segregation, race might have become irrelevant. We conceivably would live in a truly color-blind society.

The Supreme Court's self-appointed power to define what is meant by the term *liberty* under the Constitution has dramatically enlarged its supremacy and authority over the legislative branch—and thus over the people's will.

The Court's endorsement of the power flow to Washington, D.C., has all but eliminated the sovereignty of the states. Further, it has jettisoned effective checks on the power of the national government over the people of the United States.

The elimination of religion from the public sphere, coupled with Court decisions that have made it impossible for state legislatures to legislate according to the moral compass of the people, has transformed the culture and mores of our nation in just one generation.

It would be interesting to project in what ways this nation would be different today if the people had ruled instead of the Supreme Court. It is also interesting to speculate how the Founders would view the way the nation they helped to birth has unfolded.

"Every government degenerates when trusted to the rulers of the people alone," wrote Thomas Jefferson. "The people themselves, therefore, are its only safe depositories."[1] His observation about the vital importance of the people ruling reflects not only his opinion but that of all those with whom he cast his lot in 1776. If they have watched history unfold, what do they think?

More interesting is Jefferson's opinion of the judiciary as it functioned just a few decades after our nation's birth. If his fear that the judiciary was usurping the rule of the people was real in 1821, how would he view what the judiciary has done in the succeeding two hundred years?

Of course, many would question whether the opinion of Jefferson or any other Founder matters in the least. In many respects, that is what this book is all about.

THE RULE OF LAW

British journalist and essayist Walter Bagehot once observed, "The characteristic danger of great nations like the Romans and the English, which have a long history of continuous creation, is that they may at last fail from not comprehending the great institutions which they have created."[2]

The greatest institution of the American experience is the Constitution of the United States and the government created under it. It is arguable that the people of the United States no longer comprehend the Constitution. It is also arguable that they no longer expect—or demand—that they be governed by it.

Some critics contend that in the last half of the twentieth century, the courts of the United States abandoned the notion that we should be governed by the actual Constitution. Judges might make reference to it to create the appearance of legitimacy, but they then go about creating an entirely different document through discovering new and novel rights, redefining its language, and rearranging the Constitution's priorities.[3] At least one sitting judge has recently suggested that there is no reason to study the Constitution for even a second because it does not speak of today.[4]

Is that wrong? Of course, the answer depends on the one answering the question. Many citizens of the United States are content with the nation shaped by the Supreme Court. They take pride in the liberalizing of morals and the protection of new rights. They are comfortable with enhanced power in the hands of judges and in Washington, D.C. They are not concerned with what the Founders intended or what the language of the Constitution might say. They do not care how the new America came to be, for to them it is the end, the result, that matters, not the means by which America has been transformed and shaped.

But there are others, even some who may agree with the way the nation has been shaped, who are uncomfortable with the fact that it has been shaped by as few as five lawyers sitting on the Supreme Court of the United States. They do not agree that the Constitution should be reinterpreted so that the Court can bring about the result that five members believe is right.

Of the two, the second group might have the better argument if one is looking at what is the best safeguard of our liberties.

If there is anything that has made America different from other countries, it is that we are a nation of laws, not of men. That is another one of the institutions that might no longer be comprehended by the American public.

We are a nation founded on the principle that we are governed by laws and rules, not by the whim of whoever is in charge. We are all— mighty and weak, high and low, all of us—governed by the same laws and rules.

The rule of law is the cornerstone of our republic. It is the very best defense against tyranny. It is the only means by which we can hope to remain a free people.

The rule of law contemplates that the laws be known and that those who administer them have very little discretion, for too much discretion in the hands of those who administer the laws eliminates the rule of law.

It is impossible to have rule of law unless there is a fundamental law that all pledge allegiance to and agree to adhere to, and that all other laws and rules conform with. That is what the Constitution is supposed to be. It is the foundation for all other laws in our nation. It is the final and absolute check and restraint on laws and rules that infringe on our liberties and allow the government to become tyrannical.

That is why as early as 1803 Chief Justice John Marshall said that any law that was in conflict with the Constitution was void. It is important to note that he also said the Constitution was a rule for the government of the courts as well as the legislature.[5]

Because the Constitution is a written instrument, its meaning does not change. It is not a living, evolving document.

It is self-evident that in order to determine whether a law or rule is in conflict with the fundamental law of the land, the Constitution, one has to try to understand what the Constitution says and what it means. That begins with determining what those who wrote it intended it to mean. That is the only way we can assert that we live under the rule of law.

Finding the original intention is not always easy. A judgment as to what was the original intention is not always correct. Relying on the original intention does not always result in what our current society thinks is right or just.

If the people decide that the Constitution does not meet the needs of a growing, evolving nation, it must be amended, as was contemplated by those who wrote it. That is not a simple thing to do.

But the alternative is so much more dangerous.

That alternative might result in a nation whose society, culture, and values one agrees with, but it is no longer a nation under the rule of law. If the Constitution means only what five Justices of the current

Supreme Court say it means, we are not living in a nation under the rule of law. To allow the law to be decided by the whim or the discretion of five unaccountable lawyers is the opposite of the rule of law. To allow the Constitution to be given new meaning as the makeup of the Court changes is contrary to the rule of law.

Allowing the Supreme Court to decide all matters of importance in our nation carries with it another risk. There is no realistic way to correct the decision or to alter the outcome of Supreme Court decisions. Bad decisions by elected officials can be corrected—we vote in new members of Congress and a new President, and they change the law. Supreme Court Justices have no such accountability, nor do the citizens have such recourse in the Court's decisions.

The argument could be made that surrendering to the Supreme Court and allowing it to rework the laws and rules under which we live, even though those laws and rules are not in any way mandated by the Constitution, is soft tyranny. Nullifying the democratic process, denying to the people the right to decide by whom they are to be governed and the laws under which they will be governed, is soft tyranny.[6]

WHAT OF THE FUTURE?

What does the future hold if we continue under a Supreme Court untethered to the Constitution?

The death of longtime Justice Antonin Scalia, coupled with the fact that several other members of the current Supreme Court are quite elderly, has raised the specter that the Court is on the verge of being reshaped. Several legal scholars have speculated as to what the Court going forward might look like and what it might do.[7] They have ventured that a Court with a new makeup will pave new ground, revisit old issues, and possibly reverse the current Court's decisions in cases such as the ruling that there is a personal right under the Second Amendment to possess a firearm. They also speculate that a newly refashioned Court could limit the power of states to impose the death penalty or to place any restrictions on abortions. They dream of how the Court could expand the power of

Congress to regulate the lives of the American people through the commerce power, impose racial quotas, create new Constitutional rights such as the right to education, and more.

One such area that these scholars hoped the Court would revisit is the area of religious liberty. It might be worth exploring what might lie ahead for those concerned with the issue of religious liberty in the hands of a newly constituted Supreme Court.

RELIGIOUS LIBERTY VERSUS NONDISCRIMINATION

A primary transformation has occurred in our society in the arena of sexual mores. The oft-cited "sexual revolution" of the last half century has been facilitated and encouraged by Supreme Court decisions on contraception, abortion, obscenity, fornication, and adultery. The result is a culture that seems obsessed with things sexual and sex-without-consequence. It is also a culture wherein traditional morality, customs, and relationships have been abandoned by many.

The thorny problem is that not everyone has joined this revolution. There are still a substantial number of Americans who have not accepted the Court-wrought transformation of American culture. These Americans are primarily those whose opinions on morality are grounded in their religious faith. They have lived to see deeply held beliefs in traditional morality, customs, and relationships cast aside by Hollywood, the popular media, and the Supreme Court.

It is arguable that at one time such citizens exercised considerable political power in our society. In the past, they saw their elected officials at the state and national levels support traditional sexual morality and mores. The evidence of that is the abundant number of laws that were once on the books to discourage the use of contraceptives, abortion, obscenity, fornication, and adultery, as well as laws in support of traditional marriage—laws that have all been stricken by Supreme Court decisions.

But their political and social power is on the decline. Over the past few decades, they have lost most battles in the courts. They have also witnessed their view of morality practically eliminated from television and movies. Only on rare occasion do they see their values held up by Hollywood, television, or the media as positive or to be admired.

Despite the fact that they are on the losing side in the cultural revolution, they are still represented as all-powerful by those on the winning side of the culture wars. It is a convenient position for the real winners to stake out, for it allows them to continue to present themselves as the victims of an oppressive majority.

Those on the winning side of the debate have found it useful to characterize those who cling to their religious traditions in very harsh terms. The use of words such as *hater, theocrat, bigot,* and *intolerant* are not uncommon.

Among the arguments used against the traditionalists is that they "discriminate" when they refuse to accept the new morality.

It is a fact that both governments and individuals discriminate, frequently. If you don't think governments discriminate, ask a fifteen-year-old who wants to drive a car; or someone who wants to practice law or medicine but does not want to undergo the education or training required to be licensed by a state; or someone who wants to wear a badge, carry a gun, and issue tickets for speeding, even though not a certified law enforcement officer. Governments, by law and regulation, discriminate.

Personal, individual discrimination happens when we choose our friends and choose not to be friends with others, or choose a spouse and exclude all others, or when we hire one doctor to treat us and not others, or if we are the owner of a team in the National Basketball Association, when we refuse to hire a short man with no discernible basketball skills to play on our team.

It is indisputable that both people and governments discriminate. The important question is: What is acceptable discrimination, and what is unacceptable? When is it right for a government to place obstacles in the way of some? On a personal level, how much liberty do we have to associate with some, but not others?

We live in an age in which many Americans believe that it is a primary goal of government to stamp out all discrimination, that practiced by government as well as by individuals. Discrimination is viewed as the ultimate wrong. In fact, to many, the only truly wrong conduct one can engage in today is to discriminate.

A generation ago, unacceptable discrimination was basically limited to people mistreating African-Americans. It also applied to a lesser extent to those who mistreated Jews or Catholics or other religious groups. Since the middle decades of the last century, however, the number of groups that have come under the protection of the government from discrimination, by both government and individuals, has increased dramatically.

Every decision to add a new group to the list of those against whom discrimination is no longer acceptable triggers consequences, both seen and not foreseen.

The primary loser in this government effort to stamp out all discrimination on the part of individuals is personal liberty. One cannot add to the list of those groups protected from discrimination without affecting the freedom or liberty of others. One cannot demand, by force of law, equal treatment from an individual without denying that individual a portion of his or her liberty.

Absent from the public debate about what new group is now entitled to government-enforced protection from discrimination is discussion of the question, "But who will lose their liberty, their freedom to associate with whom they please, to freely exercise their religious beliefs, if this group is now to be included under the protection of the government from any type of discrimination?"

Discussion of that question in the public domain is truly needed when it involves the clash between cultural revolutionaries and religious traditionalists.

There was a time in our nation's history when a citizen was free to act as he or she saw fit, regulated by broadly accepted religious and social norms and a bare minimum of legal restrictions. Today, driven by recent expansion of artificially constructed rules regarding who is to be protected from "discrimination," we have reached the point that one philosopher deemed "the stage of ultimate inversion," wherein the government is free to do anything it pleases, while citizens may act only by permission.[8] That might be particularly true when it comes to the practice of religion in the future.

A recent report issued by the United States Commission on Civil Rights frames the issue. In its findings, this federal body stated that protecting civil rights and ensuring nondiscrimination are of "preeminent importance in American jurisprudence." It then asserted that religious exemptions to the protections of the civil rights based upon race, color, national origin, sex, disability status, sexual orientation, and gender identity "significantly infringe upon these civil rights." The commission then went on to suggest that any religious exemption from nondiscrimination laws must be defined narrowly.[9]

If, in fact, demanding nondiscrimination of groups—those currently protected or others that may be found worthy of protection in the future—is the preeminent priority, religious liberty is very much at risk.

If the only religious practice allowed in the future is that which is permitted by the government, religious liberty is but a shell of what it once was.

COURTS—THE ULTIMATE WEAPON?

Not content to have won over Hollywood and taken possession of the television screen, Internet, and other media, the advocates of the sexual revolution have now turned to the judicial system to eliminate what opposition might remain. In recent years, the conflict between the traditionalists and the revolutionaries has been waged more and more in the judicial system. Traditionalists have fallen back to the position of seeking protections from judges. On the other hand, the revolutionaries have sought the courts to eliminate those protections.

For example, a Christian student organization at a California university was denied campus status because it required its members to pledge to live traditional moral lives. When the organization sought legal protection for this right of association, the Supreme Court ruled that it was not wrong for the university to require the Christian group to accept members who rejected the Christian view of morality.

In 2014, the city of Houston, Texas, passed an equal rights ordinance banning discrimination based upon both sexual orientation and gender identity. Its critics feared it would allow adult men who identified themselves as female to enter women's restrooms. A petition drive was initiated to allow a vote to repeal the ordinance. The petition drive was encouraged by some religious leaders. When the opponents of the ordinance were refused the opportunity to put the ordinance before the people, they sued the city. In turn, in what was characterized as an effort to stifle their activities, city attorneys subpoenaed the sermons of several of the pastors who had supported the petition drive, demanding that they turn over all sermons in which they mentioned the ordinance, the mayor of Houston, homosexuality, or gender identity. Eventually, the city was forced to withdraw the subpoenas.

The Little Sisters of the Poor is a Catholic charity that serves the most destitute among us: the old, the sick, and the dying. The federal government is attempting to force the organization—an organization that faithfully adheres to Catholic teachings regarding abortion and the use of contraceptives—to abandon those teachings in the name of health-care mandates. It has been pointed out that money that could be used to help the Little Sisters' desperate patients is being expended to defend themselves from government directives. More than 100 lawsuits have been filed by different religious organizations in an effort to protect themselves from similar mandates.

A Catholic hospital chain has been sued by the ACLU because the hospitals will not perform abortions. Another Catholic service agency that operates shelters for recent immigrants has been sued by the ACLU because those shelters do not offer contraception and abortion services.[10]

If the Supreme Court is to be the final battlefield over issues of religious liberty, what might be expected?

Those who look for the Court to support their right to freely exercise their religious beliefs might not find much comfort in recent decisions and language used by the majority members of the Court.

In the majority opinion of five in the *Obergefell* case discussed in chapter 7, Justice Kennedy noted that those who adhered to the religious belief that traditional marriage was a divine precept could continue to advocate for their position and teach their principles. But in his dissenting opinion, Justice Roberts noted that the majority used the terms *advocate* and *teach* but not *exercise*. He then went on to point out the inevitable conflicts that the majority's decision would generate. He asked, what of religious colleges that refused to allow same-sex couples married student housing, or a religious organization that runs an adoption service that declined to place children with same-sex couples? He noted specifically that when asked at oral argument whether religious institutions that continued to adhere to traditional views of marriage might lose their tax-exempt status, the Solicitor General of the United States, the attorney for the United States, acknowledged that they might.

The Chief Justice noted that those and similar questions would soon be before the Supreme Court, and, "Unfortunately, people of faith can take no comfort in the treatment they receive from the majority today."[11]

Chief Justice Roberts also expressed concern with the language that the majority had used in describing the motives of those who clung to traditional marriage. He noted:

> By the majority's account, Americans who did nothing more than follow the understanding of marriage that has existed for our entire history—in particular, the tens of millions of people who voted to reaffirm their States' enduring definition of marriage— have acted to "lock . . . out," "disparage," "disrespect and subordinate," and inflict " [d]ignitary wounds" upon their gay and lesbian neighbors. . . . These apparent assaults on the character of fair-minded people will have an effect, in society and in court.[12]

In a more recent decision, Justice Alito expressed the concerns of himself and Chief Justice Roberts and Justice Thomas because they could not find a fourth member of the Court willing to consider a case out of the state of Washington. The refusal of the Court to review the decision of the Ninth Circuit Court of Appeals was deemed to be "ominous" in the words of Justice Alito.

At issue was a regulation issued by the state of Washington's State Board of Pharmacy. The regulation forbade a pharmacist from refusing to fill a prescription because of the pharmacist's religious beliefs. After a twelve-day trial, a district court judge found that the regulation had been adopted specifically to stamp out the right to refuse for religious reasons. Justice Alito pointed out that the district court found the regulations allowed the right to refuse to fill a prescription for any number of secular reasons, but punished a pharmacist who might object to being required to fill a prescription for an abortifacient. In effect, the regulation was targeted at religion and religious believers.

The Ninth Circuit reversed the District Court. An appeal was sought to the Supreme Court. Supreme Court precedent says a state cannot target religious beliefs. It is one thing for the government to refuse to protect the exercise of religion, but it is another matter for a state law or regulation to target those who attempt to exercise their religious beliefs. But, a fourth member of the Supreme Court could not be found to even consider the case, prompting Justice Alito to write: "This Court does not deem the case worthy of our time. If this is a sign of how religious liberty claims will be treated in the years ahead, those who value religious freedom have cause for great concern."[13]

It seems unlikely that the conflict between religious believers and those whose values are in disagreement with them are going to go away. It also seems unlikely that the best forum for solving those conflicts is the courts. Courts at all levels are excellent forums for declaring winners and losers. However, the conflicts between religious adherents and others cannot reasonably be solved unless there is the ability to talk and to compromise. Courts are not the best place for compromise and accommodation to be found.

There is going to remain in our nation a vast amount of diversity among the American people. Surely our nation is great enough for that diversity to survive in peace.

But if one side or the other, or both, decide that the courts are the preferred place to find a permanent and total victory over the other, the future is bleak.

Some years ago, Catholic Cardinal Francis George of Chicago predicted, "I expect to die in bed, my successor will die in prison and his successor will die a martyr in the public square."[14] Perhaps hyperbole—but the political and philosophical movement in our nation is not in the contrary direction. And the fact that someone as esteemed as a Catholic cardinal harbors such fears is an indictment of our current state of affairs.

WHAT NEXT?

This book was intended to present the case that our nation has been shaped and molded—for good or bad, depending on one's perspective—by seven major decisions of the United States Supreme Court.

This book was not intended to pass judgment on the consequences of the Supreme Court decisions, that is, the America we live in today. That is for readers to conclude for themselves.

However, the author is not agnostic on the question of whether currently or in the future our nation is better off by having an all-powerful Supreme Court, especially one that has freed itself from the constraints of the Constitution of the United States.

What concerns the author is best expressed by the written words of members of the Supreme Court in the *Obergefell* opinion.

From Chief Justice Roberts:

> The legitimacy of this Court ultimately rests upon the respect accorded to its judgments. . . . That respect flows from the perception—and reality—that we exercise humility and restraint in deciding cases according to the Constitution and the law. The role of the Court envisioned by the majority today, however, is anything but humble or restrained. Over and over, the majority

exalts the role of the judiciary in delivering social change. In the majority's telling, it is the courts, not the people, who are responsible for making "new dimensions of freedom . . . apparent to new generations. . . ."

Those who founded our country would not recognize the majority's conception of the judicial role. They after all risked their lives and fortunes for the precious right to govern themselves. They would never have imagined yielding that right on a question of social policy to unaccountable and unelected judges. . . .

The Court's accumulation of power does not occur in a vacuum. It comes at the expense of the people.

Later in the same opinion, Justice Alito observed:

> Today's decision will also have a fundamental effect on this Court and its ability to uphold the rule of law. If a bare majority of Justices can invent a new right and impose that right on the rest of the country, the only real limit on what future majorities will be able to do is their own sense of what those with political power and cultural influences are willing to tolerate. . . .
>
> Most Americans—understandably—will cheer or lament today's decision because of their views on the issue of same-sex marriage. But all Americans, whatever their thinking on that issue, should worry about what the majority's claim of power portends.[15]

The concerns expressed by those two members of the Supreme Court cannot leave those who fear the power of government breathing easier.

There are many in our nation who are content with the current state of affairs. There are many who do not share the fears expressed by Chief Justice Roberts or Justice Alito. To them, all is well.

However, those who believe that the increased power of the Supreme Court can come only at the loss of freedom to the people might be fearful of the future. To those, I encourage an escalation in their political education, involvement, and activism. Among other efforts, they must demand that only Justices who will show complete fidelity to the Constitution of the United States be nominated by our President and confirmed by the Senate.

In the end, that is our last great hope.

NOTES

Epigraph: Letter to Charles Hammond, August 18, 1821; in Spalding, ed., *Founders' Almanac*, 166.

1. Thomas Jefferson, "Notes on the State of Virginia." Query XIV, 1781.
2. Watson, *Courts and the Culture Wars*, 13.
3. See Watson, *Courts and the Culture Wars*, 4–5 for an example of such criticism.
4. Seventh Circuit Judge Richard Posner; see http://www.slate.com/articles/news _and_politics/jurisprudence/2016/08/why_courts_are_striking_down_voting_ rights_restrictions_right_now.html.
5. *Marbury v. Madison*, 5 U.S. 137,178–180 (1803).
6. For more information on the arguments for and against Originalism and Living Constitutional theories, see Berger, *Federalism;* Bork, *Tempting;* Scalia, *Matter of Interpretation;* Watson, *Courts and the Culture Wars.*
7. See Harvard Law Professor Mark Tushnet and his article found at http://balkin .blogspot.com/2016/05/abandoning-defensive-crouch-liberal.html; and the article by Erwin Chemerinsky, Dean of the College of Law, University of California, Irvine found at http://www.theatlantic.com/politics/archive/2016/04/what-if -the-supreme-court-were-liberal/477018/.
8. Author Ayn Rand said, "We are fast approaching the stage of the ultimate inversion: the stage where the government is free to do anything it pleases, while the citizens may act only by permission; which is the stage of the darkest periods of human history, the stage of rule by brute force." Ayn Rand. (n.d.). BrainyQuote .com. Retrieved November 6, 2016, from BrainyQuote.com website: https:// www.brainyquote.com/quotes/quotes/a/aynrand136316.html.
9. "Peaceful Coexistence: Reconciling Nondiscrimination Principles with Civil Liberties," briefing report by the U.S. Commission on Civil Rights, September 2016.
10. For more information about the efforts to protect religious liberty in the courts, see Eberstadt, *Dangerous.*
11. *Obergefell v. Hodges*, 135 S.Ct. 2584, 2626 (2014).
12. Ibid.
13. *Stormans v. Wiesman*, 579 U.S. ___ (2016).
14. Eberstadt, *Dangerous*, xxiv–xxv.
15. *Obergefell v. Hodges*, 2624, 2643.

ACKNOWLEDGMENTS

I would like to express my thanks to the team at Shadow Mountain Publishing for their help with this project. Thanks to Heather Ward, designer, Richard Erickson, art director, and Malina Grigg, typographer, for the striking cover and interior design and the careful layout of the text. I appreciate Chris Schoebinger, product director, and the marketing team at Shadow Mountain for their skill in getting the word out and generating excitement for the book.

Special thanks go to Jana Erickson, whose consistent expressions of faith in my writing have helped spur my efforts, and to Emily Watts, editor of this and my previous books with Shadow Mountain, whose contributions and friendship are greatly appreciated.

BIBLIOGRAPHY

INTRODUCTION

Abraham, Henry J. *Justices, Presidents, and Senators.* Lanham, MD: Rowman & Littlefield Publishers, Inc., 1999.

Bork, Robert H. *The Tempting of America.* New York: Simon & Schuster, 1990.

De Tocqueville, Alexis. *Democracy in America.* Chicago: University of Chicago Press, 2000.

Greenburg, Jan Crawford. *Supreme Conflict.* New York: Penguin Group, 2007.

Hamilton, Alexander, John Jay, and James Madison, Jr. *The Federalist.* Washington, D.C.: Global Affairs Publishing Company, 1987.

Jamieson, Kathleen Hall. *Fair and Independent Courts: A Conference on the State of the Judiciary.* September 16, 2011; available at http://www.annenbergpublic policycenter.org/Downloads/Releases/Civics%20Knowledge/Final%20 CIVICS%20knowledge%20release%20corrected2.pdf.

Ketcham, Ralph, ed. *The Anti-Federalist Papers and the Constitutional Convention Debates.* New York: New American Library, 2003.

Pritchett, Herman. "Divisions of Opinion Among Justices of the U.S. Supreme Court, 1939–1941." *American Political Science Review*, vol. 35, no. 5.

Rehnquist, William H. *The Supreme Court.* New York: Vintage Books, 2002.

Rossum, Ralph A., and G. Alan Tarr. *American Constitutional Law, Vol. 1.* Toronto: Wadsworth, 2003.

Scalia, Antonin. *A Matter of Interpretation.* Princeton: Princeton University Press, 1997.

Spalding, Matthew, ed. *The Founders' Almanac*. Washington, D.C.: The Heritage Foundation, 2002.

Toobin, Jeffrey. *The Nine*. New York: Doubleday, 2007.

Tushnet, Mark. *A Court Divided*. New York: W.W. Norton & Company, 2006.

Winneg, Ken, and Kathleen Hall Jamieson. Annenberg Public Policy Center Reports. September 28–29, 2006; available at http://www.annenberg publicpolicycenter.org/Downloads/Releases/Release_Courts20060928 /Courts_Summary_20060928.pdf.

Woodward, Bob, and Scott Armstrong. *The Brethren*. New York: Simon & Schuster, 1979.

CHAPTER 1: HOW THE SUPREME COURT BECAME SUPREME

Adams, Henry. *History of the United States*. Available at Wikisource and Henry _Adams%27_History_of_the_United_States_Vol._2.djvu/162&oldid =5801766, 5801767, and 4550002.

Charles River Editors. *The Election of 1800: The History and Legacy of America's Most Controversial Election*. CreateSpace Independent Publishing Platform, 2016.

Clinton, Robert Lowry. *Marbury v. Madison and Judicial Review*. Lawrence: University Press of Kansas, 1989.

Cunningham, Noble E., Jr. *In Pursuit of Reason*. New York: Ballantine, 1987.

EyeWitnesstoHistory.com. *Washington, D.C. 1800*. Available at http://www.eye witnesstohistory.com/pfcapital.htm.

Forte, David E. "Marbury's Travail: Federalist Politics and William Marbury's Appointment as Justice of the Peace." *Catholic University Law Review* 45:2 (1966), 349.

Library of Congress. "Religion and the Federal Government, Part 2," *Religion and the Founding of the American Republic*. Available at http://www.loc.gov /exhibits/religion/rel06–2.html.

Madison, James. *Notes of Debates in the Federal Convention of 1787*. New York: W.W. Norton Company, 1966.

Marbury v. Madison, 1 Cranch 137 (1803).

McCullough, David. *John Adams*. New York: Simon and Schuster, 2001.

Morison, Samuel Eliot, and Henry Steele Commager. *The Growth of the American Republic*. New York: Oxford University Press, 1962.

Nelson, William E. *Marbury v. Madison*. Lawrence: University Press of Kansas, 2000.

Rehnquist, William H. *Grand Inquests*. New York: Quill William Morrow, 1992.

———. *The Supreme Court*. New York: Vintage Books, 2002.

Spalding, Matthew, ed. *The Founders' Almanac*. Washington, D.C.: The Heritage Foundation, 2002.

Wilentz, Sean. *The Rise of American Democracy*. New York: W.W. Norton & Company, 2005.

CHAPTER 2: HOW THE SUPREME COURT CAME TO SANCTION RACISM

De Tocqueville, Alexis. *Democracy in America*. Chicago: University of Chicago Press, 2000.

Donald, David. *Charles Sumner and the Rights of Man*. New York: Alfred A. Knopf, 1970.

Elliott, Mark. *Color-Blind Justice: Albion Tourgée and the Quest for Racial Equality from the Civil War to Plessy v. Ferguson*. New York: Oxford University Press, 2006.

Hoffer, Williamjames Hull. *Plessy v. Ferguson*. Lawrence: University Press of Kansas, 2012.

Kendrick, Stephen, and Paul Kendrick. *Sarah's Long Walk*. Boston: Beacon Press, 2004.

McConnell, Michael W. "Originalism and the Desegregation Cases." *Virginia Law Review*, vol. 81, no. 4, May 1995.

Morison, Samuel Eliot, and Henry Steele Commager. *The Growth of the American Republic*. New York: Oxford University Press, 1962.

Plessy v. Ferguson, 16 S.Ct. 1138 (1896).

Thomas, Brook, ed. *Plessy v. Ferguson*. Boston: Bedford/St. Martins, 1997.

Woodward, Vann C. *The Strange Career of Jim Crow*. New York: Oxford University Press, 2002.

CHAPTER 3: HOW A LAW ON BAKERS' WORKING HOURS LED TO ABORTION RIGHTS

Allgeyer v. Louisiana, 165 U.S. 578 (1897).

Atkin v. Kansas, 191 U.S. 207 (1903).

Bernstein, David E. *Lochner v. New York: A Centennial Retrospective*, 83 Wash. U. L. Q. 1469 (2005).

———. *Rehabilitating Lochner: Defending Individual Rights Against Progressive Reform* (Kindle Edition). Chicago: University of Chicago Press, 2011.

Bork, Robert H. *The Tempting of America.* New York: Simon & Schuster, 1990.

Doe v. Bolton, 410 U.S. 179, 221–222 (1973).

George, Robert P., ed. *Great Cases in Constitutional Law.* New Jersey: Princeton University Press, 2000.

Griswold v. Connecticut, 381 U.S. 479 (1965).

Holden v. Hardy, 169 U.S. 366 (1898).

In re Winship, 397 U.S. 358 (1970).

Kens, Paul. *Lochner v. New York.* Lawrence: University Press of Kansas, 1998.

Lochner v. New York, 198 U.S. 45 (1905).

Morison, Samuel Eliot, and Henry Steele Commager. *The Growth of the American Republic.* New York: Oxford University Press, 1962.

Obergefell v. Hodges, 135 S.Ct. 2584, 2617 (2015).

Roe v. Wade, 410 U.S. 113 (1973).

Smith, Adam. *The Wealth of Nations* (Kindle Edition). Chicago: University of Chicago Press, 2012.

CHAPTER 4: HOW 12 ACRES OF WHEAT LED TO AN ALL-POWERFUL WASHINGTON, D.C.

Amar, Akhil Reed. "Constitutional Showdown." In latimes.com, 6 Feb. 2011.

Ashdown, Gerald G. "Federalism, Federalization, and the Politics of Crime." *West Virginia Law Review,* Spring 1996, 789.

Baker, John S., and Dale E. Bennett. "Measuring the Explosive Growth of Federal Crime Legislation." The Federalist Society for Law and Public Policy Studies, *Engage,* vol. 5, no. 2, 23; available online at http://www.fed-soc.org /publications/detail/measuring-the-explosive-growth-of-federal-crime -legislation.

Beale, Sara Sun. "Federalizing Crime: Assessing the Impact on the Federal Courts." American Academy of Political and Social Sciences (AAPSS), *Annals,* Jan. 1996.

Chen, James Ming. "Filburn's Legacy." *Emory Law Journal,* vol. 52 (2003), 1719.

Chen, Jim. "The Story of *Wickard v. Filburn:* Agriculture, Aggregation, and Commerce." Legal Studies Research Paper Series, Paper No. 2008–40.

Dimitri, Carolyn, Anne Effland, and Neilson Conklin. "The 20th Century Transformation of U.S. Agriculture and Farm Policy." Economic Information Bulletin Number 3, June 2005.

Ehrlich, Susan A. "The Increasing Federalization of Crime." *Arizona State Law Journal,* 32:825.

Garcia v. San Antonia Metropolitan Transit Authority, 469 U.S. 528 (1985).

Hamilton, Alexander, John Jay, and James Madison, Jr. *The Federalist.* Washington, D.C.: Global Affairs Publishing Company, 1987.

Hammer v. Dagenhart, 247 U.S. 251 (1918).

McCullough, David. *John Adams.* New York: Simon & Schuster, 2001.

National Federation of Independent Business et al. v. Sebelius, 132 S.Ct. 2566 (2012).

Olmstead v. United States, 277 U.S. 438, 479 (1928).

Perez v. United States, 402 U.S. 146 (1971).

Rossum, Ralph A., and G. Alan Tarr. *American Constitutional Law, Vol. 1.* Toronto: Wadsworth, 2003.

Silvergate, Harvey A. *Three Felonies a Day.* New York: Encounter Books, 2011.

Spalding, Matthew, ed. *The Founders' Almanac.* Washington, D.C.: The Heritage Foundation, 2002.

Suro, Roberto. "Rehnquist Decries Shift to Federal Courts." *Washington Post,* 1 Jan. 1999, A2.

United States v. E. C. Knight Company, 156 U.S. 1 (1895).

United States v. Lopez, 514 U.S. 549 (1995).

United States v. Morrison, 529 U.S. 598 (2000).

Wickard v. Filburn, 317 U.S. 111 (1942).

CHAPTER 5: HOW A NATION FOUNDED BY DEVOUT MEN AND WOMEN CAME TO BAN RELIGION FROM THE PUBLIC ARENA

Bellah, Robert N. "Civil Religion in America." *American Academy of Arts and Sciences,* vol. 96, no. 1 (Winter 1967), 1–21.

Engel v. Vitale, 370 U.S. 421 (1962).

Everson v. Board of Education, 330 U.S. 1 (1947).

Federer, William J. *America's God and Country.* United States of America: Fame Publishing, 1996.

Hamilton, Alexander, John Jay, and James Madison, Jr. *The Federalist.* Washington, D.C.: Global Affairs Publishing Company, 1987.

Luce, Clare Boothe. "Is the New Morality Destroying America?" *Human Life Review,* Summer 1978.

McCollum v. Board of Education, 333 U.S. 203 (1948).

Meacham, Jon. *American Gospel.* New York: Random House, 2006.

Munoz, Vincent Phillip. "The Original Meaning of the Establishment Clause and the Impossibility of Its Incorporation." *Journal of Constitutional Law,* vol. 8:4 (August 2006), 585–639.

Newman, Roger K. *Hugo Black: A Biography.* New York: Pantheon Books, 1994.

Rector, etc. of Holy Trinity Church v. United States, 143 U.S. 457 (1892).

Reynolds v. United States, 98 U.S. 145 (1878).

Rossum, Ralph A., and G. Alan Tarr. *American Constitutional Law, Vol 2.* Toronto: Wadsworth, 2003.

School District of Abington Township v. Schempp, 374 U.S. 203 (1963).

Spalding, Matthew, ed. *The Founders' Almanac.* Washington, D.C.: The Heritage Foundation, 2002.

Story, Joseph. *Commentaries of the Constitution of the United States.* Durham: Carolina Academic Press, 1987.

Wallace v. Jaffree, 472 U.S. 38 (1985).

Wolf, William J. *The Almost Chosen People.* New York: Doubleday & Company, 1959.

Zellers v. Huff, 236 P.2d 949 (1951).

Zorach v. Clauson, 343 U.S. 306, 313 (1952).

CHAPTER 6: HOW THE SUPREME COURT EMPOWERED FEDERAL JUDGES TO RAISE TAXES, MANAGE SCHOOL DISTRICTS, AND GENERALLY WORK THEIR WILL

Andrey, Gwendolyn S. "The Missing Half of Missouri v. Jenkins: Determining the Scope of a Judicial Desegregation Remedy." University of Chicago Legal Forum: Vol. 1991: Iss.1, Article 12.

Benson, Arthur. *School Segregation and Desegregation in Kansas City.* Accessed online at http://www.bensonlaw.com/kcmsd/deseg.history.htm.

Bylinski v. City of Allen Park, 8 F.Supp. 2d 965 (E. D. Mich. 1998).

Ciotte, Paul. "Money and School Performance: Lessons from the Kansas City Desegregation Experiment." Cato Institute Policy Analysis No. 298, 16 Mar. 1998.

Dunn, Joshua M. *Complex Justice.* Chapel Hill: The University of North Carolina Press, 2008.

Easton, Robert E. "The Dual Role of the Structural Injunction." 99 Yale L.J.1983, June, 1990.

Employers Ins. of Wausau v. St. Clair Contractors, Inc., 2007 WL 1202378 (D. Idaho, 2007).

Hamilton, Alexander, John Jay, and James Madison, Jr. *The Federalist.* Washington, D.C.: Global Affairs Publishing Company, 1987.

Missouri v. Jenkins, 495 U.S. 33 (1990).

Missouri v. Jenkins, 515 U.S. 70, 126 (1995).

Parkman, Chelsey. "*Missouri v. Jenkins:* The Beginning of the End for Desegregation." 27 Loy.U.Chi.L.J. 715 (1996).

Spalding, Matthew, ed. *The Founders' Almanac.* Washington, D.C.: The Heritage Foundation, 2002.

CHAPTER 7: HOW THE SUPREME COURT PLAYED A CENTRAL ROLE IN REDEFINING THE VALUES AND CULTURE OF AMERICA

American Civil Liberties Union v. Mukasey, 534 F.3d 181 (2008) and 555 U.S.1137 (2009).

Ashcroft v. American Civil Liberties Union, 535 U.S. 564 (2002).

Ashcroft v. The Free Speech Coalition, 535 U.S. 234 (2002).

Baker v. Nelson, 93 S.Ct. 37 (1972).

Bowers v. Hardwick, 106 S.Ct. 2841 (1986).

Carey v. Population Services International, 97 S.Ct. 2010 (1977).

Eisenstadt v. Baird, 92 S.Ct.1029 (1972).

Goodridge v. Department of Public Health, 440 Mass. 309 (2003).

Griswold v. State of Connecticut, 85 S.Ct. 1678 (1965).

Jenkins v. Georgia, 94 S.Ct. 2750 (1974).

Joseph Burstyn v. Wilson, 72 S.Ct. 777 (1952).

Lawrence v. Texas, 539 U.S. 558 (2003).

Martin v. Ziherl, 269 Va. 35 (2005).

Miller v. California, 413 U.S. 15 (1973).

Mukasey v. American Civil Liberties Union, 555 U.S. 1137 (2009).

Mutual Film Corporation v. Industrial Commission of Ohio, 35 S.Ct. 387 (1915).

Obergefell v. Hodges, 135 S.Ct. 2584, 2598 (2015).

Reno v. American Civil Liberties Union, 521 U.S. 844 (1997).

Sweeny, JoAnne. "Undead Statutes: The Rise, Fall, and Continuing Uses of Adultery and Fornication Criminal Laws." *Loyola University Chicago Law Journal,* vol. 46 (2014), 127–73.

United States v. Playboy Entertainment Group, 529 U.S. 803 (2000).

United States v. Various Articles of Obscene Merchandise Schedule, 709 F.2d. 132 (2d Cir. 1983)

United States v. Windsor, 133 S.Ct. 2675 (2013).

Woodward, Bob, and Scott Armstrong. *The Brethren: Inside the Supreme Court.* New York: Simon & Schuster, 1979.

CONCLUSION

Berger, Raoul. *Federalism: The Founders' Design.* Norman: University of Oklahoma Press, 1989.

Bork, Robert H. *The Tempting of America.* New York: Simon & Schuster, 1990.

Eberstadt, Mary. *It's Dangerous to Believe.* New York: Harper, 2016.

Marbury v. Madison, 5 U.S.137 (1803).

Obergefell v. Hodges, 135 S.Ct. 2584 (2014).

Scalia, Antonin. *A Matter of Interpretation.* Princeton: Princeton University Press, 1997.

Spalding, Matthew, ed. *The Founders' Almanac.* Washington, D.C.: The Heritage Foundation, 2002.

Stormans v. Wiesman, 136 S.Ct. 2433 (2016).

Watson, Bradley C. S., ed. *Courts and the Culture Wars.* Lanham, MD: Lexington Books, 2002.

INDEX